Marja Peltola & Ann Phoenix

# Nuancing Young Masculinities

## Helsinki Boys' Intersectional Relationships in New Times

HUP HELSINKI UNIVERSITY PRESS

Published by
Helsinki University Press
www.hup.fi



First published in 2022

Cover design by Ville Karppanen
Cover photo by Ole Schwander / iStockphoto.com

Print and digital versions typeset by Siliconchips Services Ltd.

ISBN (Paperback): 978-952-369-066-0
ISBN (PDF): 978-952-369-067-7
ISBN (EPUB): 978-952-369-068-4
ISBN (Mobi): 978-952-369-069-1

https://doi.org/10.33134/HUP-16



The full text of this book has been peer reviewed to ensure high academic standards. For full review policies, see http://www.hup.fi/

VERTAISARVIOITU
KOLLEGIALT GRANSKAD
PEER-REVIEWED
www.tsv.fi/tunnus

Suggested citation:
Peltola, M. and A. Phoenix. 2022. *Nuancing Young Masculinities: Helsinki Boys' Intersectional Relationships in New Times*. Helsinki: Helsinki University Press. https://doi.org/10.33134/HUP-16.

To read the free, open access version of this book online, visit https://doi.org/10.33134/HUP-16 or scan this QR code with your mobile device:

*To a new generation of children who are helping to nuance gender relations and young masculinities in new ways, particularly Aavi, Kimaya and Oula.*

# Table of Contents

# Tables and Images

## Tables



## Images

# Transcription key

| Element | Meaning | Example |
|---|---|---|
| . or , | Break in utterance | Well I don't know, maybe. Maybe it's just more that, I can't really, I guess it might be because my father is more, he spends more time with us and so it might be because of that. |
| – | Utterance stops abruptly | Are there other differences, like, are they like differ–? |
| … | Hesitation or hedging in speech | Yes but… here you see quite many of them. |
| (…) | Omitted material | Quite a lot even play FIFA, or a couple. (…) It is hard to say. |
| [] | Nonverbal communication<br><br>Explanation of the context<br><br>Overlapping speech | Probably about friend groups. [laughs]<br><br>What is it [the unmanly deed] here?<br><br>Jaakko: There's more water in us yeah. [Daniel: Yeah.] |

# Acknowledgements

The research that informs this book would not have been possible without the award of the Jane and Aatos Erkko guest professorship (2016–18) to Ann Phoenix. We are particularly grateful to the Jane and Aatos Erkko Foundation for their generosity and to the Helsinki Collegium for Advanced Studies (HCAS), University of Helsinki, for awarding the guest professorship together with Marja Peltola's postdoctoral fellowship. The Collegium provided invaluable support for our research, including by providing some time for Malin Fransberg to work on the project and enabling the HCAS interns to translate the research interviews conducted by Marja Peltola. Particular thanks are due to Sami Pihlström and Sari Kivistö, who enabled the extension of the professorship into the second year and were unfailingly interested in, and supportive of, the research.

Our greatest thanks go to the young people who gave their time to discuss their ideas on masculinities, gendered relations and everyday life with each other and with Marja Peltola. It would not, however, have been possible to interview them without the permission of the three schools and youth club in which Marja worked and of the young people's parents. Many thanks to all of them.

The book was completed during the 2020–21 COVID-19 pandemic when schools closed and we both spent a lot of time working at home. Marja thanks her colleagues in the Social Studies in Urban Education research unit, at the Faculty of Educational Sciences in the University of Helsinki, and in the Unit of Social Research at Tampere University, for warm collegiality and support with distance working. Marja also thanks Immu for sharing the load at home, and Aavi and Oula for their invaluable presence that helps her to concentrate on what is essential.

Thanks also to colleagues in the GEPS (Gender and Pedagogical Processes in Society) research group at Umeå University, particularly Ann-Louise Silfver, Eva Silfver and Ulrika Widding, who provided enjoyable physical and then virtual contexts for work, discussions and conviviality while hosting Ann as the Kerstin Hesselgren guest professor. As always, Charlie Owen provided delicious lunches and dinners as well as company, and so much more than usual, during the COVID-19 pandemic.

CHAPTER I

# Young Masculinities: Contention, Complexity and Contradictions

In the millions of words written about the pandemic that entered global consciousness in 2020, masculinities featured in contradictory ways. On the one hand, some commentators expressed concerns that the characteristics of masculinity make boys and men poorly suited to managing the pandemic well. They were considered at risk of poor mental health, of breaching lockdown and behavioural restrictions and of committing violent acts on women and children (Burrell and Ruxton, 2020; Deuchar and Goulden, 2020; European Commission, 2021; Glick, 2020). On the other hand, some researchers reported that lockdown offered opportunities for a shift in how men and boys see themselves and so a shift towards more egalitarian masculinities and gender-equal relations (Mwiine, 2020; Wenham, Smith and Morgan, 2020).

The study reported in this book was conducted before the pandemic; however, the observations above illustrate two important points about masculinities that lay the groundwork for this book. First, that there is no one version of masculinity that all boys or all men subscribe to. Masculinities are plural and can and do change over time, dependent on the sociostructural context. Equally, COVID-19, together with the global impact of the Black Lives Matter movement, has underscored that boys and men are viewed and treated differently, and have very different experiences, depending on how they are racialised. Second, COVID-19 helped to illuminate the ways in which contexts, identities, practices and social change are always interrelated. In order to understand masculinities, therefore, it is more important than ever to understand boys' and men's everyday practices, the identities they take up, and their varied positioning in the institutions in which they are located, their localities, nations and the globe. This book makes a contribution to that understanding by presenting a detailed picture of boys of different ethnicities, from different urban localities, who attend schools in Helsinki, Finland.

It is not that masculinities first came to public attention during the coronavirus pandemic. Indeed, they have long been part of public consciousness and debate in such negative ways that it has become normative to think of masculinities as problematic and as in crisis. For boys in many societies, that crisis has, for decades, been about poor educational attainment in relation to girls, their disengagement from schoolwork, denigration of girls, homophobia, propensity for violence and coping strategies that hinder help-seeking and self-care (Arnesen, Lahelma and Öhrn, 2008; Frosh, Phoenix and Pattman, 2002; Janssen, 2015). This constellation of features is part of what has been dubbed 'toxic masculinity' in media and popular discussion (Flood, 2018), to signify that it is bad both for women and for men. It is damaging to girls and women because they are subject to sexist behaviours, including abusive or violent treatment, and to boys and men because it constrains their relations with women, children and other boys and men as well. This does not mean that all men and boys are disadvantaged since men still occupy the most senior positions in most societies (Kramer and Harris, 2020). Indeed, 'toxic masculinity' reinforces and produces gender inequalities that disadvantage women and privilege men. However, while 'toxic masculinity' is a catchy term that has enabled much public discussion on problems of certain masculine behaviours, it has also been criticised for individualising social problems and treating them in a decontextualised and ahistorical way (de Boise, 2019). At the same time, as society and girls and women have changed around them, boys and men are sometimes seen as 'becoming the "new" victims in society' (Haywood et al., 2018: 1).

These contradictory notions of masculinities 'in crisis', as 'toxic' and men and boys as 'victims' alert us to the fact that we have to think about masculinities in complex, plural ways if we are fully to understand them.

Masculinities are further complicated by their production both in microprocesses, as in the classroom or at home, and macro-processes linked to structural contexts such as nations, racialisation, social class and region (Kimmel, 2017). Gender does not, therefore, provide a total explanation for the patterning of masculinities. Boys' educational attainment cannot, for example, entirely be related to gender, but varies by ethnicity, social class and nation (Gross, Gottburgsen and Phoenix, 2016). Masculinities have repeatedly been shown to be racialised around the globe (Mac an Ghaill and Haywood, 2014; Phoenix, 2008). Any examination of masculinities thus has to be intersectional, considering commonalities across boys and men in different contexts and differences between boys and men in the same contexts, as well as attending to boys' own perspectives.

This book focuses on boys and masculinities but does so in ways that recognise that neither are free-floating. Instead, they are situated in specific contexts and relate to particular boys with specific histories who are part of global gendered politics (Hearn, 2004). It contributes to an understanding of the shared features of masculinities among boys while showing how local contexts differentiate boys and masculinities. It also includes the voices of a few girls since gendered practices are relational, involving girls and women as well as boys and men. The book contextualises contemporary young masculinities in Finland, a national context where relatively little research has been done on boys and masculinities (with notable exceptions being Huuki, 2010a; Manninen, 2010; Lunabba, 2013; Kivijärvi, Huuki and Lunabba, 2018). This book is informed by a study, *Masculinities and Ethnicities in New Times*, conducted in 2017 and 2018, that focused on the negotiation of masculinities and ethnicities in an era when Finland is renegotiating its national self-identity as a multi-ethnic country. The study explored the narratives of 12- to 15-year-old boys and girls, of different ethnicities, living and attending schools in Helsinki, the capital of Finland, at the end of the 2010s.

This chapter introduces and explains the background to the issues that inform the book. It sets the scene by first drawing on the literature to show why it is crucial to take a nuanced view of masculinities if we are to move forward debates on the 'crisis' of masculinity and better understand masculinities. We engage critically with the contradictions in the literature, presenting both international and Finnish literature on what we currently know about boys and masculinities. The first section addresses the question 'What are masculinities?' by focusing on the development of the concept of 'hegemonic masculinity' and related theorisations as a key framework for helping researchers to think through, and analyse, masculinities. The chapter then introduces other theoretical issues that inform the analyses in the chapters that follow, particularly intersectionality and racialisation, and finally discusses briefly the national and local context in Helsinki, Finland, where the study was conducted.

## Theorising Masculinities: Situated and Performative Hegemony

Theorisation of masculinities has burgeoned over the last 20 years, partly because they have become a source of anxiety in many societies. For boys, concern has focused on their poor educational attainment in relation to girls, their disengagement from schoolwork, their propensity for violence and (re)production of power hierarchies (Arnesen, Lahelma and Öhrn, 2008; Cann et al., 2021; Hall, 2020; Janssen, 2015; Keddie, 2020, 2021). A pervasive element of such research findings is that what boys and men feel able to do is intimately interlinked with what they consider constitutes masculinity. While, as discussed above, boys and men are positioned in different ways in relation to normative conceptions of masculinity, they are constrained and/or buttressed by what they imagine 'real' men and boys should be like (Laberge and Albert, 1999; Majors and Billson, 1993). This leads many researchers to employ the notion of 'hegemonic masculinity' as a conceptual lens.

Since 1985, the Australian gender scholar Connell (1989, 1995, 1998, 2016) has been the most influential researcher in the field of hegemonic masculinity. Connell's central argument is that masculinity is an active and dynamic project produced from both a personal trajectory and the social resources available. It is relational in that it is constructed in relation to other men as well as to women, and hierarchical, with power relations being a vital part of its construction. Carrigan, Connell and Lee, when first coining the term in a 1985 paper, drew on Gramsci's (1971) concept of hegemony. Gramsci identified and explained the complex process whereby a social group (the bourgeoisie) can maintain consent for its rule through both domination and intellectual and moral leadership and, at the same time, have its leadership taken for granted and rendered invisible because it defines social norms. While the term 'hegemonic masculinity' has become ubiquitous, Connell recognised that it is very difficult to attain and so only a minority of men and boys can either claim hegemony or be recognised as hegemonic. Its hegemony, therefore, requires that men and boys who fall outside the category hegemonic masculinity position themselves in relation to it.

Connell (1995) identified four types of masculinities. Hegemonic masculinity is the masculine ideal, associated with heterosexuality, toughness, power and authority, competitiveness, and the subordination of gay men. Marginal masculinity describes men who embody some traits associated with the hegemonic masculine ideal and may even be considered 'hypermasculine' but lack the institutional and economic power that characterises hegemonic masculine privilege (e.g. men of colour, working-class men). Complicit masculinity describes the large number of men who cannot fit the hegemonic ideal but do not challenge the hegemony. Lastly, subordinate masculinity describes masculine 'others', e.g. gay men. Of these, hegemonic masculinity comes to dominate others and to become normative, defining social understandings of ideal masculinity and the desires of many men and boys. According to Connell, many men aspire to the hegemonic ideal even if they feel that they cannot attain it, so it is important to the fantasy lives of many men. Since it is unattainable for many, it is often parodied, critiqued or subverted as men position themselves in relation to it.

While many researchers eschew the notion of 'types' of masculinity as being too fixed and essentialist, the concept of hegemonic masculinity has continued to be debated, used and contested (often simultaneously) in the research literature. This is partly because it has helped to further understanding that masculinities are plural, dynamic, socio-economically located and in competition with each other (as well as with femininities). In addition, it clarifies how it is that the constituents of hegemonic masculinity continue to be reproduced across generations. As it has gained popularity, however, it has been subjected to much critical scrutiny. In the field of masculinities studies in Finland, the concept of hegemonic masculinity was adopted immediately after Connell and colleagues coined the term, in the 1980s, and has continued to be influential. In a critical review of how masculinities are understood in the Finnish field of masculinities studies, Hyvönen (2020) pointed out that the concept of hegemonic masculinities is applied flexibly and used together with poststructuralist elements, such as Butler's notion of performative gender. Hyvönen suggested, however, that the concept is too often used for explaining 'all kinds of actions of all kinds of men' (ibid.: 50), and in ways that are not sensitive to differences between men and the local and situation-specific varieties of masculinities.

A further problem is that the hegemonic category is itself plural rather than singular. As early as the 1990s, Cornwall and Lindisfarne (1995) argued that both macho and 'new' men can be hegemonic, while Bjerrum Nielsen and Rudberg (1994), in their study on gender in school, identified a 'clan' of intellectual boys who, by consent, dominated their Oslo school without being tough or sporting. This is something also found in later work by those who suggest that there are now inclusive forms of masculinity where homophobia and 'homohysteria' have significantly decreased and boys are not taunted with name-calling if they are homosocial (Anderson, 2009; Anderson and McCormack, 2018). This 'theory of inclusive masculinity' has created academic interest, but also raised serious criticism from many, among them de Boise (2014: 324), who pointed out that, since hegemonic masculinities are flexible and historically mobile, 'it may be the case that what Anderson calls "inclusive" is just another hegemonic strategy for some heterosexual, white, middle-class men to legitimately maintain economic, social, and political power in the wake of gay rights'.

Discussion on 'inclusive masculinity' can be understood as a part of a broader academic discussion on 'hybrid masculinities', which refer to 'men's selective incorporation of gendered performances and elements of identities associated with marginalized and subordinated masculinities and femininities' (Bridges and Pascoe, 2014: 246; Demetriou, 2001). However, most scholars utilising the concept of hybrid masculinities do not consider that 'new' or hybrid masculine practices challenge gendered power hierarchies and inequalities but perpetuate them. Bridges and Pascoe (2014) argued, in line with de Boise (2014: 324), that hybrid masculinities illustrate 'the flexibility of identity afforded privileged groups' such as white, heterosexual men. They argue that this flexibility helps to sustain masculine hegemony by obscuring it at a time when the legitimacy of patriarchy is increasingly being questioned. The concept of hybrid masculinities therefore focuses on the flexibility of, and changes in, hegemonic masculinity rather than suggesting that masculine hegemony in itself is challenged by men. The concept of 'caring masculinities', instead, proposed by Karla Elliott (2016), is an attempt to theorise forms of masculinities that reject domination and relational hierarchies that are at the heart of theories of hegemonic masculinity. 'Caring masculinities' are based on incorporation of care into masculine identities and valuing positive emotions deriving from caring, interdependency and relationality. Elliott (2016) suggested that supporting such values would help to decrease the costs of masculinity for both men and women, and advance gender equality. However, it remains an open question how widespread such masculine identities are and how best to advance them.

Another set of criticisms of the notion of hegemonic masculinity relates to the situatedness of the impact of the characteristics associated with hegemonic masculinity. Men may gain power in some ways and in some places, but not in others. For example,

Edley and Wetherell (1995) pointed out that some working-class men who apparently have hegemonic characteristics are much less socially powerful than middle-class men who do not share those characteristics. Similarly, Majors and Billson (1993) argued that a 'cool pose' can be used defensively by African American men to protect themselves from being overwhelmed by the racism they face and by their lack of social power. Yet, there are costs because the 'cool pose' can distance them from their relationships and feelings. Thus, adopting characteristics of hegemonic masculinity does not guarantee a hegemonic position in all aspects of boys' and men's lives. Indeed, while the concept of hegemonic masculinity requires physicality for its expression, it functions in imprecise and abstract ways, because it is embodied by very few boys and men. These observations relate also to the perspectives of Hearn and Blagojević (2013), who analysed patriarchies as trans(national) and intersectional, Beasley (2013), who pointed out that hegemonic masculinities include elements that are not necessarily embodied in the same people, and Howson and Hearn (2019), who showed that, for these reasons, in the field of Critical Studies of Men and Masculinities, hegemonic masculinity is an empty signifier that obfuscates the construction of the conflicts it entails.

These and other reformulations of masculinities have enabled the 'reconfiguration of hegemonic masculinity to include aspects of the once subjugated masculine stereotype of the nerd' (Kendall, 1999) such as 'geek ascension', in which there is a 'complex negotiation of outsiderhood and privilege, even outsiderhood as privilege' (Bell, 2013: 79). With the increasing importance of digital living, for example, some men previously stigmatised as 'geeks' are able to gain ascendancy and engage in overtly misogynistic, sexualised banter that resists gender equality and converges with hegemonic masculinity (Ging, 2019). Ironically, therefore, it seems that claims (and displays) of a subordinate masculinity can serve as moves in the construction of more hegemonic identities, just as the (outward) display of machismo can be glossed as undermining its authenticity as an identity for 'ordinary' men. The 'doing' of masculinities, it seems, is always in the detail (Wetherell and Edley, 2014: 359.) Thus, in analysing the hegemonies of real men and boys, it becomes apparent that what would generally be viewed as subordinate masculinities can function hegemonically in particular contexts and that displays of hegemonic masculinity can be used to undercut hegemony.

Despite the criticisms, many researchers continue to use the term hegemonic masculinity because they find evidence of a pervasive and powerful form of masculinity that is pre-eminent and desired and that frames boys' and men's behaviour and aspirations (Lee, 2004; Oeur, 2018). At the same time, the features of hegemonic masculinity are recognised both to have changed and to be susceptible to political change towards gender equality, as well as to have maintained various of its features (Haywood et al., 2018). The concept of hegemonic masculinities has been reformulated in ways that take account of the criticisms made of it and that fits with conceptualisations of identities as multiple, fragmentary, and variable (Rattansi and Phoenix, 2005).

Connell (1995, 1996, 1998) has never taken an essentialist view of masculinity, but has theorised masculinities as culturally specific, collectively produced, relationally sustained, dynamic and multilayered (and hence potentially contradictory). She views masculinities as about material and discursive gender and power relations and positioning in a gender order. In other words, masculinities are about patterns of practice, often embodied by men. Christensen and Jensen (2014) argued that the criticisms made of hegemonic masculinity come from the ways in which Connell's work has been picked up, rather than the formulation per se.

In response to the criticisms of hegemonic masculinity, but its continued use, Connell and Messerschmidt (2005) reformulated it as geographically located (locally, regionally and globally) and underlined the importance of embodiment to the concept. They also highlighted its symbolic nature, in which hegemony works through symbols or signifiers such as particular everyday practices or modes of dress that symbolise and command authority since few boys and men are able to consistently embody hegemonic masculinity. In recognition that gender relations are always arenas of tension, Connell and Messerschmidt also gave recognition to the dynamism of hegemony: that masculinities are always in process. There are simultaneously transformations and stasis in masculinities in relation to feminisms and expectations of gender equality, shifts in identities and what a 'good life' means, and decline in 'masculine' industries and jobs. There are, therefore, simultaneously 'old' and 'new' masculinities in lived contradiction. Messerschmidt (2018, 2019) argued that hegemonic masculinities are both 'hidden in plain sight' (2018: 74) and ubiquitous and proposed that they should be seen as a 'structured action theory' that incorporates a focus on both social structures and discourses and so enables analyses of the power relations he considered that notions of 'inclusive masculinity' neglect.

This is in keeping with the ways in which, at the turn of the 21st century, Wetherell and Edley (1999: 351–352) succinctly summarised fruitful ways to conceptualise hegemonic masculinity.

> What seems worth keeping (…) is the notion of hegemonic forms of intelligibility – the notion that men's conduct is regulated by shared norms of sensemaking which are consensual although contested, maintain male privilege, which are largely taken for granted and which are highly invested. What we can't accept, however, is the common assumption that hegemonic masculinity is just one style or there is just one set of ruling ideas (most often understood as macho masculinity). Rather, there is a multiplicity of hegemonic sense-making relevant to the construction of masculine identities, and in addition these forms of sense-making do not always seem to regulate through their unreachable and aspirational status.

Yang (2020) suggested that, if hegemonic masculinity is not filled with pregiven meanings and content, it is possible to recognise that gender is relational and to envision its hopeful, transformative potential.

Hearn (1998: 18) pointed out that the notion of masculinities itself is increasingly subjected to scrutiny for being imprecise and too multifaceted in referring to 'institutional patterns, behaviours, identities, experiences, appearance, practices, subjectivities'. In the Finnish context, Kondelin (2016) criticised research for treating men/boys and masculinities as (almost) inseparable, which does not enable the examination of femininities in men and boys, for instance. Following Waling (2019), Hyvönen (2020) also argued that, while the power hierarchies in boys' and men's lives are important, the current terminology and how it is applied in Finnish masculinities studies do not capture those parts of boys' and men's lives that lie outside struggles for status and hegemonic masculinities.

These discussions highlight the ways in which understandings of masculinities, as well as masculinities themselves, have changed. We may be said to be in what Hearn and his colleagues (2012: 37), from a review of Swedish literature, called a 'third phase' of masculinity research. This they saw as having moved beyond notions of hegemonic masculinities to diversity and critique. In thinking about the hegemony of real boys and men, as Hearn has long advocated, it is important to recognise that, alongside moves towards more inclusive masculinities for some boys, there have been other developments that produce, in new forms, some of the most pernicious elements of masculinist power relations (Nicholas and Agius, 2018). Wetherell (1998) developed the concept of 'troubled subject position' to indicate that masculinity is a practical accomplishment in which boys and men negotiate complex 'troubled' and 'untroubled' subject positions and power relations in talk. The notion of 'troubled subject position' alerts us to the relational affects and emotions that are produced and circulate as masculinities are negotiated in everyday practices (de Boise, 2018; Reeser and Gottzén, 2018). These responses to situations and the world may never be owned, recognised and named as particular emotions (Wetherell, 2012) but they have powerful impacts on boys' identities and practices. They are also precarious in that, as Majors and Billson (1993) suggested, 'doing' hegemonic masculinity can make men vulnerable. Indeed, since hegemonic masculinity is unattainable for most boys and men, it may function as 'cruel optimism' (Berlant, 2010), something desired that is an obstacle to boys' and men's flourishing (Allan, 2018). In that context, Way (2019) welcomed the decision of the American Psychological Association to recognise 'adhering to norms of masculinity (…) as a risk factor for boys' and men's mental health'. She viewed this as helping mental health professionals to understand the dangers of masculine stereotypes that demean desires for empathy and connection as 'girly and gay'.

From the discussion above, it is clear that masculinities are not natural and pregiven but are 'performative', in Judith Butler's terms, produced and negotiated as boys and men 'do masculinity' in different contexts and at different times as 'normalizing regimes of practice' (Martino and Pallotta-Chiarolli, 2003). Butler (1990: 173) conceptualised social categories, such as gender, as embodied through a process of performativity, which involves fantasy and an ongoing discursive process of 'citing' gender norms that are normalised in society. Gender comes to seem naturally occurring because it is continuously and performatively reiterated. People come to occupy and claim social categories such as masculinities, therefore, through repetitive performances.

Based on what we have discussed in this section, in the analysis that follows we utilise the concept of hegemonic masculinities, understood as plural, intersectional, locally negotiated and 'done' in interaction. The 'doing' of hegemonic masculinities is negotiated by boys and men in ways that take up, reproduce, create and resist subject positions that are multiple and can be 'troubled' or 'untroubled' (Wetherell, 1998). 'Doing boy' is always situated, contextual and politically located. This fits with one of the central arguments made by Hearn (2004), who argued that it is preferable to focus on the hegemony of actual men and boys and the study of multiple forms of hegemony in the gender order, rather than a general hegemonic masculinity. It is, therefore, important to draw on concepts that enable theorisation of masculinities to recognise its dynamic plurality, its imbrication in power struggles and that it is thoroughly psychosocial, situated in local, regional and national contexts. The section below discusses 'liveable lives', intersectionality and racialisation – concepts that, together with notions of hegemonic masculinities, enable the complexity of young masculinities to be captured. The meanings that boys make from their gendered, racialised practices can be viewed as central to the process of crafting liveable, intersectional masculinities.

## Liveable Intersectional Masculinities: Making Gendered, Racialised and Local Meanings

The discussion above underlines the point that different versions of masculinities are not equal. Hegemonic masculinities are centrally linked with discourses of the normative. Butler (2004) suggested that discursive constructions of gender give recognition to some ways of living and everyday practices and so make them normative and part of 'liveable life'. Those constructions not recognised in this way are constructed as non-normative and outside cultural discourses of what it is to be a person, as having 'unbearable lives'. According to Butler (2004), autonomy and subjectivity are constrained by normalising processes, with the result that those constructed as having 'unbearable lives' have to assert claims to liveable (or bearable) lives. For many boys, the negotiation of hegemonic masculinities includes fear of failure, dread and shame. Allan (2018: 181, 187) suggested that:

> So much of masculinity (…) is based on a fear of being revealed as being a fraud. Put another way (…) men seem to fail a lot at being masculine (…) Masculinity, I argue, resides in a cruel optimism that highlights not only the shame of masculinity, but also the dread that is felt in having been shamed, being shamed, and the possibility, if not promise, of being shamed once more and again.

It may be that Allan is overstating the case that masculinity is predicated on failure. Nonetheless, it has repeatedly been shown that boys pre-emptively defend themselves against fears of not being viewed as sufficiently masculine (Frosh et al., 2002; Way, 2004). Many boys, therefore, in Butler's (2004) terms, find their autonomy and subjectivity constrained by normalising processes and have to act in ways designed to claim bearable lives. The differences between boys can, therefore, increase their vulnerability in that there are many versions of masculinities that change over time and context in which boys and men can position themselves, even within the same interactions. Positioning in some versions of masculinities opens the possibility that boys will be constructed outside the normative.

In order to capture this plurality, dynamism and complexity, in this book we employ the concept of intersectionality to foreground the fact that everybody is simultaneously positioned within multiple social categories, such as gender, social class, nationality and 'race' (Crenshaw, 2017). Intersectionality reminds us that we can only fully understand the category of masculinity by viewing it as decentred by other social categories such as racialisation, social class, age and nation (Phoenix and Pattynama, 2006).

Intersectional theory has gained popularity partly because it allows an engagement with the complexity and multilayered nature of everyday life and social categories (Anthias, 2020; Collins and Bilge, 2020; Yuval-Davis, 2011). Equally important, it is a heuristic reminder that all categories are associated with power relations (Brah and Phoenix, 2004; Lutz, 2015). Christensen and Jensen (2014: 60) brought together hegemonic masculinities and intersectionality to suggest that an intersectional approach offers a 'theoretical tool for analyzing the complexities of differences and hierarchic power relations between men' and, in a parallel way, boys.

An intersectional approach conceptualises social categories as 'situated accomplishments' (West and Fenstermaker, 1993). The ways in which they are experienced and treated is not natural and pre-ordained but expressed within particular social contexts and relational. The social categories analysed as intersecting are themselves dynamic and socially constructed. This is captured in the terms ethnicisation and racialisation, which treat ethnicity and race as 'done' in particular contexts at particular times and as involving change over time, rather than being fixed and permanent. Racialisation, as theorised by the Martiniquan psychiatrist and anticolonial political theorist Frantz Fanon (1967), is the process by which 'race' becomes imbued with meanings and socio-economically structured. It is both dynamic and saturated with meanings.

While the study that informs this book was conducted predominantly in schools, this is not a study that foregrounds masculinity in schools or boys' academic attainment. Instead, we explore the diversity of contexts and relationships in which young people do masculinities and the range of relations they negotiate in doing so, including school, leisure time and hobbies, gaming, friendships and family lives. The research discussed below addresses two main questions: What meanings do young people make of masculinities? How do they craft identities and liveable lives from masculinities and the intersections of masculinities with ethnicities, place and space amongst other things? It therefore focuses on young people's narratives as a window into the meanings they make.

Narrative analysis is premised on the understanding that we 'make' and account for ourselves through autobiographical narratives (Bruner, 1990, 2003). Narratives are *stories* of experience, not straightforward descriptions of events (Squire, 2008). Riessman (2008) pointed out that narratives often emerge with contradictions, particularly between how lives ought to be ideally lived and how they really are or between what is taken for granted as normative and the non-normative. A narrative approach is, therefore, ideal for understanding the diversity of young people's negotiations of their positioning within normative constructions of masculinities and the meanings and identities they make in the process within their cultural contexts (Bamberg, 2004). A close focus on what people actually say recognises heterogeneity, complexity and ambiguity of settings and agents.

> [I]f we take the time to understand how members of society use culture to interpret and represent their own and others' lives, we stand to diversify what it means to become who and what we are. In the process, we glean a more culturally nuanced and narratively active understanding. (Gubrium, 2006: 250)

> In paying close attention to how men talk about themselves (and others) as men, we gain a clearer sense of how masculinities are created, negotiated, and deployed. (…) [T]he picture here is one of dynamism and complexity. Any attempt to pin men down or to classify them into types is usually frustrated. However, in embracing this complexity, not only do we gain a better (and more ecologically valid) feel for the texture of social life, but we

> also end up with a stronger understanding of how gender hierarchies are constructed, unsettled, and sustained. (Wetherell and Edley, 2014: 362)

It is that stronger understanding identified by Wetherell and Edley that we aim to present in the pages that follow.

## Studying Masculinities in Helsinki Schools

There is now a substantial body of research on boys and masculinities that contributes to crisis thinking. Yet, much research also serves to counter simplistic thinking either that all boys are the same, or that boys, particularly black and working-class boys, are straightforwardly responsible for their conceptualisation as 'toxic' (Ferguson, 2000; Pinkett and Roberts, 2019; Way and Chu, 2004). These contradictions signal the need for more work on boys and masculinities. There is an even greater need for systematic research in changing times. This chapter opened by thinking about the need to understand masculinities in the changed times ushered in by the global changes produced by COVID-19 and Black Lives Matter. The 21st century is, however, characterised by other changes that are expressed in particular ways in the countries and political systems in which young people live (Gottzén, Mellström and Shefer, 2019; Ingram, 2018; Langa, 2020). In this section, we briefly introduce some of the patterns of contemporary social change that are central to the Finnish context and particularly Helsinki, where the study *Masculinities and Ethnicities in New Times* was conducted.

Finland is one of the Nordic welfare states, and national identity in Finland is strongly attached to notions of Nordic welfare egalitarianism and high achievements in gender equality (e.g. Keskinen et al., 2009). According to Holli and Kantola (2007), international comparative studies show the relatively high success of both the Finnish women's movements and 'state feminism' between 1969 and 1999 but, since the turn of the millennium, the developments seem to have been more contradictory. New tools for achieving gender equality have the potential to be transformative but suffer from problems of implementation and lack of resourcing (ibid.). However, in Finland gender equality is at times viewed as already achieved, a finished project. This line of thinking serves to obscure the persistent gender inequalities manifest in many spheres, such as in the prevalence of gender-based violence and harassment (e.g. Julkunen, 2010).

Given that this book is written in English, it is crucial to note a gendered language issue that is specific to the Finnish language and particularly relevant to translation of discussion of gender into English. That is that the third person pronoun *hän*, equivalent to both 'she' and 'he', is gender-neutral in Finland – although this is not related to equality policies. As a result, we have struggled to translate some of the expressions used in the interviews, where the gender of the people talked about is implied in the context, but not in the actual terms used. The difficulty is that the English translation requires more gender specificity unless the plural 'they' is used or the more formal and more archaic 'one', which is highly unlikely to appear in young people's talk.

Besides the notions related to gender equality, the myth of (historical) monoculturalism is another central constitutive part of Finnish national identity (Tervonen, 2014). This notion has been shown to be mythic and, since global migration movements are transforming Finnish society, Finland is becoming more visibly multi-ethnic and linguistically plural. Finland does not collect population data on ethnicity or 'race' (only on countries of birth and first languages), and therefore long-established ethnic minorities – such as the Roma, the Sami and part of the large population with Russian ancestry – remain invisible in the statistics. The population statistics therefore offer only a very rough (under)estimate of 'multi-ethnicity' in Finland. The percentage of the population 'of foreign origin' – as people both of whose parents were born outside Finland (regardless of whether or not they themselves were born in Finland) are labelled by Statistics Finland – remains rather low and was just under 7 per cent in 2020. However, a comparison with 1990, when the comparable percentage was 0.8, illustrates the marked societal change. This trend is expected to continue in future decades. A large part of the minoritised ethnic group population lives in the cities of southern Finland. Helsinki, where this study was located, is among the most 'multi-ethnic' cities in Finland, with roughly 17 per cent of Helsinki residents having parents categorised as 'foreign-born' (Official Statistics of Finland, 2021). As with migration flows everywhere, immigration to Finland is greatest from neighbouring countries, especially from Russia and Estonia. The next largest migrant populations come from Somalia and Middle Eastern countries.[1]

The increased visibility of ethnic and linguistic plurality requires rethinking of the borders of Finnishness. As in other countries where migration has produced rapid visible change in the ethnic composition of nations, there are contrary reactions, in terms of opposition and acceptance (Harinen et al., 2012). In this process, the notion of 'Finnish' gender equality also functions as one of the tools for excluding those who are constructed as racialised and cultural others (Honkasalo, 2013; Keskinen, 2018). At the same time, antiracist feminist (mostly activist) voices have also grown stronger (Keskinen, 2018). However, generally the gender equality politics and discourses in Finland tend to be treated separately from the politics and discourses on diversity, in terms of ethnicity, 'race' and sexuality. This separation is reflected even at the level of legislation, where the Act of Equality between Men and Women regulates gender-based discrimination, while the Non-Discrimination Act regulates discrimination based on all other categories (Holli and Kantola, 2007).

While increasing multi-ethnicity and 'rediscovering' Finland's multicultural history have changed the way Finnishness is understood at least from the 1990s onwards, this negotiation was particularly notable in Finnish media discussions at the time this study was conducted in 2017–18. These discussions were fuelled by the so-called 'refugee crisis' of 2015, when for some months Finland, like many other European countries, received a greater

---

[1] The third and fourth largest groups of 'population of foreign origin' in Helsinki have their backgrounds in Somalia (11 per cent) and Iraq (6 per cent) ('Population with Foreign Background in Helsinki', 2021).

number of asylum-seekers than customarily had been the case due to the emergencies in Syria and Afghanistan (e.g. UNHCR, 2015). Keskinen (2018) suggested that the term 'refugee crisis' is a misnomer in Finland. She argued that, instead of being a 'refugee crisis', 2015 and its aftermath was a 'crisis of white hegemony' in Finland, when many segments of the society felt threatened by the sense that the link between national identity and whiteness was being eroded. The relatively minor shift in the ethnic composition of the Finnish nation was followed by events that exercised the nation: in Helsinki in 2016, a member of a neo-Nazi group assaulted a man who later died, and in Turku in 2017 there was a knife attack in a crowded marketplace by a man with Jihadist motives. These events attracted high media visibility and heated public debate, bringing ethnicity and racism to wider public consciousness than would otherwise have been the case. These issues were, therefore, likely to have been at least remotely familiar to our research participants at the time of the interviews.

In addition to broader societal changes and media discussions, local environments such as schools are highly significant to the everyday lives of children and young people. In the study of *Masculinities and Ethnicities in New Times*, schools were also important locations because the data collection was largely conducted in school settings. The Finnish education system has been developed with egalitarian ideals in mind. The nine years of comprehensive school are compulsory for all (from seven to 16 years), and approximately 86 per cent of young people receive an upper secondary school certificate, with about half of them gaining a vocational qualification and half attending a general academic upper secondary school. The comprehensive school, with its stated task of guaranteeing a high-quality education and eligibility for further studies to everybody, has been one of the flagships of the Finnish welfare state and a source of national pride (e.g. Ministry of Education and Culture, 2020) and global attention (Bastos, 2017). However, the vast literature on inequalities in education in Finland shows that egalitarian ideals are not entirely achieved in the schooling system, since social class, ethnicity, 'race' and migration background, as well as ability/disability, continue to shape both educational trajectories and the everyday experiences of differently positioned children and young people (e.g. Kilpi-Jakonen, 2014; Kosunen et al., 2020; Kurki, 2019; Souto, 2011).

Gender is a recurrent theme in public discussions on equality in schooling in Finland. In line with the international 'boy crisis' talk, concerns have been raised on boys' lack of engagement with schooling, which is reflected in (slight) gender differences in learning results attained (PISA15; PISA18) and with a smaller proportion of boys and young men in general academic upper secondary schools and in higher education, in comparison with girls. Forty-six percent of boys applied to general academic upper secondary school as their first choice after comprehensive school, compared with 65 per cent of girls (Finnish Institute of Health and Welfare, 2021). Gender scholars have pointed out that this public discussion tends to treat both boys and girls as homogeneous groups and, in highlighting the differences between boys' and girls' school performance, bypasses the heterogeneity of masculinities for boys in school contexts as well as rendering invisible those girls who struggle with schooling (e.g. Arnesen et al., 2008; Lunabba, 2018). It is also noteworthy, although not generally considered in public discussion on gendered differences in Finnish PISA results, that boys are found to fare 'better' than girls on several measures of well-being: they are more often content with their lives, feel less anxiety than girls, and report feeling better connected than girls with the school community (Välijärvi, 2017).

In addition, the 'boy crisis' does not manifest equally among boys, due to the global changes that have restructured labour markets, causing a decline in 'traditional' male-dominated blue-collar work (e.g. Kosonen, 2016; McDowell, 2012; Ward, 2015). In keeping with the rest of the affluent Minority World, these have increased the plurality of school-to-work trajectories in Finland, disadvantaging some boys and men over others. As a result, even though working-class masculinities are particularly associated with disengagement from school and schoolwork, it has long been recognised that working-class masculinities, like all masculinities, are plural (Kosonen, 2016; Roberts, 2013). This was first identified in Paul Willis's classic 1977 research on working-class masculinities, which showed that some working-class boys were highly engaged with schoolwork (the 'ear'oles').

Social class has been a rather muted topic in Finnish society, since the welfare project and educational expansion have fuelled the erroneous idea that Finland has achieved its egalitarian goals and that social class differentials have, therefore, become minimal and redundant (Kolbe, 2010; Tolonen, 2008). Research continues to show, however, that it has remained significant in shaping educational and wider life trajectories and well-being in multiple ways, perhaps increasingly so (e.g. Erola, 2010; Kivinen et al., 2012). While social class identifications are not necessarily clear and some people abandon them altogether (Kahma, 2010), research among young people shows its persistent significance both for biographies and at the level of everyday hierarchisation and border work based on embodied and lifestyle markers of class (Käyhkö, 2006; Peltola, 2021; Tolonen, 2013).

Within the last 20 years, trends of urbanisation and socio-economic segregation have been identified as further challenges for realising equal educational opportunities in urban areas. This parallels the inequities found in many major cities in Europe and elsewhere, although the polarisation is not as great in Finland (Vaattovaara et al., 2018). Residential areas in Helsinki, for instance, have remained socio-economically heterogeneous, but 'spatial concentrations of deprivation', which used to be small dots on urban geographers' maps, are expanding and forming larger clusters (ibid.). Ethnicised and racialised minorities tend to live in marginal areas, so that socio-economic segregation largely overlaps with ethnic segregation. For schools, this means that students have divergent everyday realities (Bernelius and Vaattovaara, 2016; Kosunen et al., 2020). Even though Helsinki is among the most ethnically diverse areas in Finland, large 'white pockets' remain where white Finnish young people have very little contact with people of other ethnicities either in school or in the areas they regularly frequent (Peltola and Phoenix, 2022). It should be noted that, since this study was conducted in different residential areas in Helsinki, we are able to present some of the differences between these urban areas but unable to analyse differences in the intersections between masculinities in urban and rural contexts (see Armila, Käyhkö and Pöysä, 2018 on boys in rural Finland).

Little is currently known about what the most recent changes in the ethnic composition of Finnish society mean for young people's everyday practices. It is clear, however, that young people have to negotiate new social orders in relation to more multi-ethnic social environments, which are differentiated by gender and social class (Tolonen, 2017). As Haywood and colleagues (2018) pointed out, concerns about crises of masculinities are much more likely in times of social change. For Finnish boys, threats of violence, physicality, materiality and gendered performances (as in 'fear power') have been found to be used strategically as resources, to gain respect and to affect power relations in schools (Manninen, Huuki and Sunnari, 2011). Yet, masculinities are changing in Finland, as in many societies. For example, problematic drinking cultures and their connection to a particular way of being masculine are, partly, giving way to more heterogeneous masculinities and femininities in drinking practices (Törrönen and Roumeliotis, 2014). While caring and showing vulnerability remain hard to reconcile with being masculine among boys (Huuki and Sunnari, 2015; Peltola, 2020), caring and emotions have become central themes in studies on masculinity (Elliott, 2016) and fatherhood in particular (Eerola, 2014).

The study of boys and masculinities that we report below contributes to the intersectional and contemporary understanding of boys' everyday cultures and gendered relations. In keeping with current thinking about masculinities, it attends to boys' imaginaries of masculinities in changing times. These imaginaries are patterned by inequalities in national societies as well as boys' identities and aspirations (Tarabini and Ingram, 2018). They also impact on how boys negotiate everyday social orders of who is respected, valued and denigrated as masculine (Tolonen, 2017). The ways in which boys from different ethnic groups imagine masculinities as well as negotiate their masculine positioning are thus a central focus of this project. Schools are also a central site for the (re)production of masculinities (Ingram, 2018; Reichert and Keddie, 2019). In the chapters below, our focus is on how Finnish young people 'do' intersectional masculinities in their narratives, fitting with what Hearn and colleagues (2012) call the 'third wave' of masculinity studies.

## The Chapters that Follow

**Keeping Context in View: The Study and the Helsinki Schools (Chapter 2).** This chapter sets the context for the chapters that follow by first describing the methodology of the study and the schools that constitute the context in which boys of this age spend much of their time. It shows how the methods used facilitated the analyses of the substantive findings and explains how the study was conducted with a view to getting a holistic picture of masculinities in 12- to 15-year-olds. The second part of the chapter considers the school and leisure contexts of the study participants.

**Hegemonic Masculinities and Constructions of Gender Differences (Chapter 3).** This chapter begins the process of interrogating the concept of hegemonic masculinities by documenting the ways in which young people in Helsinki schools negotiate hegemonic masculinities in groups and in dyadic conversation with a researcher. It examines the ways in which boys differentiate themselves from girls and how the few girls interviewed think about this.

**Violence, Popularity and Constructions of Plural Masculinities (Chapter 4).** In this chapter, we unpack some of the elements of hegemony that are much debated in the literature by examining narratives on popularity. We start by looking at the role of violence in boys' relationships and go on to look at their narratives about popularity, which indicated that they considered that popularity is not based on violence, or fear of it, but likeability and being 'funny'.

**Homosocial Relationships: Peers and Friends (Chapter 5).** This chapter focuses on the ways in which boys' social relations with their peers were patterned. Boys were generally committed to maintaining inclusive masculine friendships within their school classes. It was important to many that 'boys are friends with all boys'. This positive norm of sociability did not mean, however, that friendships were intimate or confiding. Very few boys felt they could confide in their friends and those few who said they could were highly selective about who they confided in and what they confided.

**(Dis)identification with Representations of Masculinities (Chapter 6)**. With the help of photo-elicitation, this chapter illustrates commonalities and differences in the kinds of images of masculinity boys found attractive, likeable and disliked.

**Family Relationships (Chapter 7)**. This chapter draws predominantly on the individual interviews to consider participants' accounts of relations negotiated at home. It presents the story of participants' relationships with their mothers, fathers and siblings. It first examines boys' narratives of their gendered relationships with their mothers and their fathers, then considers whether they report themselves to be open with their parents about what they are thinking and things they do. The last section considers their relationships with their siblings.

**Narratives of Multiculturalism (Chapter 8)**. This chapter engages with the ways in which the young people in the study were thinking about, and learning to live, multicultures and multiculturalism. As with their narratives of gender differences, young people presented egalitarian multicultural ideologies while also normalising white Finnishness and minimising racism.

CHAPTER 2

# Keeping Context in View: The Study and the Helsinki Schools

This chapter sets the context for the chapters that follow by first describing the data and methodology of the study and then the study schools. It explains how the study was conducted with a view to getting a holistic picture of masculinities in 12- to 15-year-olds (rather than simply their lives at school). The chapter shows how the methods used facilitated the analyses of the substantive findings.

The latter parts of the chapter describe the main contexts in which the research material was gathered, the three schools. They also present other relevant elements of the young people's everyday lives, such as their extra-curricular activities. These contexts, and the social relationships and social orders that are interlinked with them, are important for contextualising the key themes analysed from the interviews and discussed below. It would, for example, be difficult to understand the boys' negotiations of their positions in their school hierarchies, and their descriptions of 'acceptable' masculinities in relation to teachers, other adults, girls and boys, without understanding how these were situated in their schools and everyday lives. The participants made clear that space and place are both important for 'doing' young masculinities. For instance, they often drew distinctions between their previous and current schools and between different classes in the school year.

## Data and Analysis

The interview material from the study was gathered among sixth- to eighth-graders in three comprehensive schools and one youth club in Helsinki during 2017 and 2018. This age group – 12- to 15-year-olds – is transitioning from childhood to youth and, in the Finnish school context, from primary school (sixth grade) to lower secondary school (grades seven to nine). This often means broadening social environments and increased importance of peer relationships, which makes negotiations of masculinities and other identities in this age particularly significant (see also Frosh, Phoenix and Pattman, 2002).

Most of the young people (28 of the 32) were interviewed in the schools. The recruitment strategy was designed to include young people from different social class and ethnic backgrounds. To that end, schools in three different residential areas were selected. One school – pseudonymised as 'Nurmi School' – was located in a wealthy (upper-)middle-class area, and the pupils in this school were almost exclusively white Finns. 'Kukkula School' was located in an area that was socio-economically mixed and had a minority (approximately one fifth) of pupils with so-called 'foreign backgrounds'. The third school – 'Harju School' – was located in a socio-economically less affluent area and had a larger proportion of pupils from backgrounds other than Finnish. While the three schools provided fruitful contexts for contacting a diverse range of young people, extra-curricular clubs can enable young people to view social issues in different ways from those possible in mainstream school (Keddie, 2020; Orellana, 2019). For that reason, we contacted two Helsinki youth clubs and were able to involve one, 'Keinu', in order to increase the diversity of the participants. Keinu youth club was located in a somewhat impoverished area.

### *Organising Interviews*

Overall, there were 32 participants in the study. Marja Peltola conducted all the discussions and interviews (which were all in Finnish). These consisted of seven focus group discussions with between two and five participants in them (two mixed gender and five with only boys) and 22 individual interviews. Twenty-seven of the participants were boys, and four were girls. One participant identified as a boy but had previous experience of living as a girl and was still often misgendered as one. The majority of the interviewees – 22 – were white Finns. Three were mixed parentage and both parents of six participants had been born outside Finland, in Eritrea, Estonia, Ireland, Italy, Korea, Nepal, Russia, Somalia and the United States. The background information of the participants, separately for focus group interviews and individual interviews, is presented in Tables 2.1, 2.2 and 2.3.

**Table 2.1:** Number of participants in focus groups and individual interviews at each age.

| Age | Focus groups | Individual interviews |
|---|---|---|
| 12 | 11 | 7 |
| 13 | 8 | 7 |
| 14 | 4 | 6 |
| 15 | 3 | 2 |
| Total | 26 | 22 |

**Table 2.2:** Gender of participants in focus groups and individual interviews.

| Gender | Focus groups | Individual interviews |
|---|---|---|
| Boy | 22 | 21 |
| Girl | 3 | 1 |
| Trans | 1 | |
| Total | 26 | 22 |

**Table 2.3:** Participants' racialised and migrant backgrounds.

| Background | Focus groups | Individual interviews |
|---|---|---|
| White Finnish | 20 | 13 |
| Mixed parentage (with one Finnish parent) | 3 | 3 |
| With parents who migrated to Finland | 3 | 6 |
| Total | 26 | 22 |

The participants were of different ages in the different schools. In Nurmi School, the participants were recruited from two parallel seventh-grade classes (12–13 years), in Kukkula School from one eighth-grade class (14–15 years) and in Harju School from one sixth-grade class (12 years). In all classes, all pupils were offered the possibility to participate in the study, thus no pre-selection was made by the teachers or the researchers. In each school, the focus groups were first conducted with those pupils who themselves and whose parents had given written consent for them to participate. The participants were then offered the possibility to have individual interviews as well. It was also possible to participate in an individual interview only. Ten interviewees participated in a focus group interview only, six participated in an individual interview only, and 16 participated in both. The focus groups were formed partly according to the participants' wishes (e.g. friends together) and partly according to the teachers' suggestions and depending on who had returned the parental consent form in time. At the youth club, 'Keinu', the two 15-year-old interviewees were contacted by a youth worker at the researchers' request.

By and large, our study was regarded in the schools and at the youth club with positive interest by the teachers, youth workers and young people alike. The teachers organised time slots for us to introduce the study to the pupils and hand out the parental consent forms. Some of the pupils also asked questions on the project at this point. A common experience in all three schools was that most girls in the classes did not consider taking part in a study on masculinity inviting or relevant to them. Consequently, only four girls participated in the study, three of them in mixed-gender focus group discussion (but not in individual interview) and one in individual interview (but not a focus group). Interest in the study did not always easily translate into participation among boys either (see also Elliott and Roberts, 2020). For example, in one class, a group of boys said from early on that they would be prepared to participate in the study, but they kept 'losing' the parental consent forms (sometimes finding them again in the bottom of their bags) and requesting new ones or explaining that they had forgotten to present them to their parents. Two boys in this group eventually returned the consent forms and participated in the individual interviews, while the other two did not. Another small group of boys, invited to participate in the study at another youth club, remained more reserved towards the study despite meeting with the researchers a couple of times. One brought back a completed parental consent form but did not give it to the researcher because the other boys did not bring back their forms. In consequence, interviews were never done in that youth club.

Some of the boys initially reacted to the focus groups with nervous curiosity and joking, but in most cases the participants engaged seriously in the discussions and, when asked afterwards, said that they considered the interview themes meaningful and that they appreciated being asked their opinions. The interviews were very different in nature. In one all-boy focus group, we interpreted the constant joking and carnivalising of the interview situation as a way for the boys to cope with a situation that they considered potentially risky in terms of maintaining their social positions in their social hierarchies. In a mixed-gender group of two boys and two girls, discussion proceeded in good spirits and the participants avoided absolutist categorisations related to gender. Yet, gender organised both where they sat and how turns were taken in the discussion (Peltola and Phoenix, 2018). Given that we conducted only one mixed-gender focus group in school and one in the youth club, it is not possible to compare the groups on gendered positioning etc. While the gender composition is bound to affect the interaction, many other issues played a role. In individual interviews, joking did not feature and serious reflection on the themes seemed to be easier, including for those for whom the focus group had been negotiated through flippancy and light-heartedness. The individual interviews also allowed space for reflection for those (altogether three) boys who, in the focus group, were noticeably more silent than the others. However, in the individual interviews, the participants varied in terms of how deeply they were willing to consider the themes and the vocabularies on which they drew in order to do this (see also Elliott and Roberts, 2020; Frosh et al., 2002).

In the schools, the interviews took place during class time and so the schools' temporal and spatial organisation set limits for the interviews. In two schools, the length of the school classes was 45 minutes, and the interviews needed to be finished by the time the break following the class ended (within 60 minutes), although some focus groups took a little longer. In one school, the classes lasted for 90 minutes, which allowed more flexibility, and the interviews lasted between 30 and 90 minutes. The focus group discussions were often, but not always, slightly longer than the individual interviews. The teachers who had volunteered to cooperate with the project organised a space for the interviews, often in empty classrooms, meeting rooms, computer/printing rooms and storage rooms. In many cases, it was not easy to find a quiet space where an interview could be conducted without interruption: teachers sometimes popped into the classrooms to look for material they needed for the class next door, meeting rooms were sometimes reserved for additional classes or meetings with students, teachers sometimes came to printing rooms to collect their printing and retrieved items from storage rooms, not knowing we were there. These interruptions were sometimes highly disruptive and sometimes minimal. The greatest disruptions were those that required us to move rooms (three cases). While the discussion continued after the disturbance, it was difficult to recapture what was about to be said before the interruption. The interviewees seemed to consider the interruptions and requests to change room a 'normal' part of school life – they provoked no signs of surprise or complaint, although sometimes they elicited jokes. In the school settings, the pupils seemed to be used to their physical presence being controlled by teacher actions, rules and spatial constraints. At the youth club, the interview took place in one of the recreational rooms without interruptions.

Ethical issues were considered throughout the research process. Ethical clearance was received from the University of Helsinki, the Divisions for Education (schools) and Culture and

Leisure (the youth club) of the City of Helsinki and the principals of each school, as well as the leaders of both youth clubs approached. Focus groups and interviews were only conducted if parents gave written permission. With the young people, their consent was negotiated and confirmed before and at the beginning of the interviews, when Marja explained the ethical principles related to confidentiality in handling the data and that the interviewees would be pseudonymised (all names appearing in the text are pseudonyms). In conducting the interviews, Marja took care not to put the young people in situations that would make them feel awkward, embarrass them or result in social sanctions for them afterwards or conflicts in their social relationships. For instance, in the focus group interviews, we avoided intimate questions addressed to one participant only, and we let the participants choose whether they wanted to participate in both an individual and a focus group discussion, or in only one of these.

### *Focus Groups and Individual Interviews*

The objective of the focus group interviews was to enable the young people collectively to produce narratives on masculinity and being a boy or a girl in school and in young people's lives generally. The objective of the individual interviews was to enable more individual narratives in a situation in which peer influence was not as acutely present as in the focus groups. Following Allen (2005), we understand both group discussions and individual interviews as social settings where both what is said and how masculinity is *performed* through talk and other communication in the interview situation are relevant.

One of the benefits of conducting both focus group discussions and individual interviews is that they illuminate different everyday practices. The individual interviews allowed the young people to say things they would not say in a group and enabled them to talk confidentially and think about doing masculinities, including, if they wish, in ways that run counter to constructions of hegemonic masculinities (Frosh et al., 2002). The focus groups enabled insights into both the breadth of issues encompassed in the topics of discussion and the ways in which these are negotiated across boys or boys and girls (Barbour, 2018). The combination also enabled the interviewer to meet most of the interviewees more than once and thus to get to know them a little better. Both the focus groups and the individual interviews were semi-structured and guided by an aide-mémoire summarising the central interview themes, which included school and its social hierarchies, differences among boys, differences between boys and girls, leisure time and hobbies, (social) media, friendships, (multi-)ethnicity and family.[2] The order, length and depth of discussing these themes varied from one interview to another. The interview questions were tailored to suit the interview situation and the interviewees' stories and styles (Elliott and Roberts, 2020); for instance, some more quiet interviewees grew more engaged with the interview, particularly since they were able first to talk about issues they had a special interest and expertise in. The individual interviews included a photo-elicitation task, where the participants were presented with 21 photographs carefully chosen to represent different versions of masculinities and asked which they liked, which they disliked, which they identified with and would not wish to be like as well as which they considered manly and unmanly. The photo-elicitation as a method is discussed in more detail in Chapter 6, where its findings are presented.

As is always the case in studies based on interview material, the accounts and narratives in the data are co-constructed and influenced by the interview context (Mann, 2016). The interviewer, Marja Peltola, is a white Finnish woman in her late 30s (at the time of the data gathering), and this position inevitably had an impact on interactions in the interviews – as does all positioning. The boys performed their masculinities in relation to each other and girls in general, but also in relation to the female interviewer. In their study with a very similar interview procedure, but with

[2] The interview procedure and the themes roughly paralleled the procedure and themes in the study *Young Masculinities* (Frosh, Phoenix and Pattman, 2002).

a male interviewer, Frosh, Phoenix and Pattman (2002: 36–38) reported that the boys said that they would not have shared their stories in the same way had the interviewer been female and that 'all-male' interviews contributed to the boys investing in asserting themselves against girls. While the boys said this, it may not necessarily be the case that they would have shared less if they had been faced with a female interviewer. Niobe Way (2011: 80), in her study of boys' friendships, found that shared gender (and ethnicity) did not necessarily produce a more 'open and honest' atmosphere in interviews, as performing 'proper' masculinity may make expressing vulnerability harder with a male interviewer. While it is important to reflect on the interviewer's gender and its consequences for the interaction in the interview situation, a simple preference for 'matching' positionality is misleading and unable to take into account the dynamism of social positions and their intersectionality (Elliott and Roberts, 2020; Gunaratnam, 2003). The analyses below include analysis of the performative dynamics of an interview situation that illuminated the ways in which the boys did masculinity in relation to the woman interviewer (see Chapter 3). In addition, the interviewer's position as an adult and an academic researcher was sometimes commented upon by the interviewees – usually by emphasising the difference between the interviewer and the interviewee and sometimes questioning the interviewer's ability to 'get' the everyday life of young people. For instance, Lauri, when asked who his favourite artists were, started the list by saying, 'you probably haven't heard about any of them', and Kristian assumed the ironic position of an 'interpreter' or cultural broker who 'translates' the slang terms used by another boy in the same focus group, talking indirectly to the researcher by saying things like 'that means a joke, if there is a doctor present who doesn't know what that means'. The whiteness of the interviewer, although not commented on, possibly made it harder for the interviewees who were from racialised minority ethnic groups to disclose and analyse experiences of racialisation and racism and may have led white participants to take their perspectives on multiculturalism for granted (see Chapter 8).

## *The Analysis*

The Finnish-language interviews were transcribed and then translated into English.[3] The translations were checked against the original transcriptions and recordings by Marja Peltola and Ann Phoenix checked the English idioms. Marja also wrote field notes on the focus group discussions and pen portraits of each individually interviewed participant, which summarised the key themes in the interview together with her subjective observations and impressions on the atmosphere in the interview.

We began the analysis of the first focus group interview by reading the whole interview together out loud line by line and using the analysis of one line to anticipate what we expected to happen next in the transcript. This method was developed from Marine Burgos's (1991) notion, drawing on Paul Ricoeur's narratology, that narrators have the difficult task of unifying heterogeneous material into coherent narratives so that there is always a struggle when people start telling stories. Even if they are not aware of it, Burgos argued that conflicts are often evident at the start of stories, as are the key issues that animate people's narratives and the subjective positions that narrators take up in relation to their subject matter. She therefore advocated line-by-line sequential narrative analysis of the kind we conducted on the first interview. Making predictions enabled us to identify and explore the prejudgements that we made about how the story would unfold and to foreground any impulses to skate over meanings and puzzles (Wengraf, 2001).

Line-by-line reading is an intensive and extremely time-consuming method and thus it was not possible to employ this method of analysis for the whole corpus of the data. Instead, we continued reading interviews out loud, but drawing on longer chunks of the transcripts. This still enabled us to stop to think and discuss whenever we were puzzled about what the young people

[3] The translations were made by Linda Sivander, Olli Heiniö and Anna Koivukoski as part of their internships at the Helsinki Collegium for Advanced Studies in 2017–18. We are very grateful to all three for their valuable help and to the Collegium for funding this.

meant, to ensure that we shared understandings. We analysed both the researcher's questions and the participants' responses and comments in this way, on the basis that social interactions are co-constructions where comments and questions produce particular possibilities for response and new narratives (Frosh et al., 2002). After each reading session, the central themes emerging in that particular interview were summarised on a large sheet. This practice made it easier to see which themes began to be repeated in the data, which narratives and themes were unique, and how the different themes related to others in the same interview and across all interviews.

## School Contexts

Since almost all the interviews were carried out in comprehensive schools, the school contexts are important for the understanding of young people's locally negotiated social orders (see e.g. Hoikkala and Paju, 2014; Tolonen, 2001). Like all schools in Finland, the three schools were co-educational (mixed gender) and, like almost all comprehensive schools with very few exceptions, they were free of charge and followed the core national curriculum. While it is possible to make a special application to attend a school in a residential area other than where one is living, as a general rule school enrolment is on the basis of residence, so many children and young people attend their local schools. Therefore, it can be assumed that the demographics of the pupil body in the schools we visited largely reflected the demographic composition of the three different residential areas where they were located. This does not, however, remove the possibility that the young people who agreed to participate within the schools were unrepresentative in some way. School performance indicators are not made public in Finland, due to concerns that they will indirectly lead to school segregation (Wallenius, 2020), and thus cannot be described here.

The physical spaces of the concrete school buildings and the age-based grade system structure social relations and interaction in schools. The participants recruited from grades six, seven and eight were differently positioned, according to their (slightly) different ages, in the grade hierarchies of the schools. In Finland, the division between the primary school (*alakoulu*, grades one to six) and lower secondary school (*yläkoulu*, grades seven to nine) was officially dissolved in 1999 and grades one to nine together form the basic Finnish education. Despite this, the division between primary and lower secondary schools is still often reflected in the school buildings and how the space is organised. Further, it remains a central way for adults and children alike to divide the nine years of comprehensive schooling in Finland. Entering lower secondary school is considered one of the milestones towards more 'mature' status and away from (early) childhood. Additionally, there were local, school-specific ways to organise grades that also had significance for the social relations and divisions in the schools. While pupils in different grades did not necessarily socialise with each other, the participants did compare themselves and others with the pupil groups present in the same space.

**In Nurmi School**, the participants were recruited from the seventh grade and were 12- to 13-year-olds. The school building where they studied only had grades seven to nine, which meant that in the autumn period of seventh grade, when the interviews were conducted, all the participants had very recently changed schools and were the youngest in their school. This made the theme of changing schools important in the interviews. There was a widely shared understanding among the pupils interviewed that the current school was 'better' than the primary schools where the participants had gone in earlier years – and, indeed, better than most schools in Helsinki. This understanding was partly produced by contrasting the current school with more regulated everyday life in primary schools, but also reflected the good 'reputation' the school had among parents, and, in addition, related to the school's location in a very (upper-)middle-class and white area (see also Kosunen, 2014). The teachers were considered nice and, being 'subject teachers' instead of 'classroom teachers' as in the lower grades, better qualified pedagogically for teaching specific subjects. The school was also considered freer than the earlier school(s) in terms of how pupils were expected to behave, what they could do during the breaks and when they were allowed to use mobile phones. Thus, many considered that they had a more mature role, with greater freedom and responsibilities.

The recent change of schools meant getting to know many new people, but also a need to negotiate group formations and social hierarchies anew. The acceptable, 'hegemonic' and inferior forms of masculinity were also redefined and negotiated, in relations between the teachers and the pupils, in relations between boys and girls, and among different boys. For instance, in a focus group discussion with two boys, Valtteri described his old and new schools and, at the same time, positioned himself in the school hierarchies.

> MP: If many came here from [a local primary school], and then you came for example from [another school] so do you get into this like, like quite well into the group regardless?
>
> Valtteri: Yeah quite well you can get into, like at least I haven't been beaten up once or anything like that.
>
> MP: Did you expect that, maybe you'd be beaten up here?
>
> Valtteri: They don't beat people up here, there aren't those kind of people. In primary school there were quite a lot of those kind of people who always beat each other up. (*Focus group 4, 2 boys, 12 years, Finnish background, Nurmi School*)

Performing masculinity is an integral part of Valtteri's narrative, as he spoke in a light-hearted manner about 'not having been beaten up' in the new school. It is noteworthy that, while the new school is described in a positive way through the absence of a violent ethos, violence still acts as a central category in relation to which Valtteri constructed his masculinity. At the same time, he fine-tuned his position by distancing from both the position of a victim and that of a perpetrator of violence.

As implied in the extract above, the social dynamics among boys and girls in Nurmi School were also influenced by the fact that a large proportion (but not all) of the pupils had previously gone to a particular local (primary) school. This meant that those who came from the same local school knew and had a long, shared history with several people from their current class and the parallel classes. In contrast, those who had previously gone to other schools, local or further away, were a minority and had not necessarily known anyone from the school beforehand. While this did not seem to be either a 'good' or 'bad' thing in terms of the social hierarchies, it meant that the effort needed for creating social connections and friendships was greater for those pupils who came from other schools.

**In Kukkula School**, the participants were recruited from the eighth grade and were 14- to 15-year-olds. This school was organised in a way that departs from the division between primary and middle schools and there were younger pupils studying in the same building with the lower secondary school graders. All the interviewees had studied in the same school for at least three years and only seldom made any comparisons between their current and previous schools. The division between the primary and lower secondary school was much less pronounced in the interviews with the pupils of this school. Generally, the interviewees considered the school 'nice', 'good' or 'nothing to complain about'. According to them, most of the teachers were rather good, although some were better than others. The participants were not, therefore, similarly invested in representing the current school as a very good one or better than any other schools, as the participants in the Nurmi School were, but by and large they were content with it.

The interviewees – who were recruited from the same class – all suggested that, in their own class, all boys got along well with each other, while girls were considered more or less self-segregating. Quite strong distinctions were made between their own class and the parallel classes, which were described as more restless and including more 'troublemakers'. While 'boys getting along with all the boys' was a repeated theme, the boys in the class were divided into two groups – closer friendships were formed within these groups and the sociability and friendliness between members of the two groups seemed to stay at the level of getting along. The pervasive influence of shared schools was demonstrated by the fact that the dividing line had been produced by the merging of two local schools some years back.[4] At that point, the class had received a number of new pupils, who together formed a group of their own. Even though the change was not recent, it was referred to in several interviews, both by those who had originally studied in the school in question and by those who had entered the school after the merging.

MP: What kind of groups are they then?

Martin: In our class, the guys from [the other school in the area] and then those not from [the other school in the area].

MP: So there were many of you who came from [the other school on the area] at the same time?

Martin: Five [boys] if you count me, no wait. Yes, five if I am counted in, too.

MP: So the, the difference is that the others came from another school. Are there other differences, like, are they like differ–?

Martin: They like different things than others so they are not very social with others, except for when they ask for a pencil or something. (*Individual interview Martin, 15 years, Estonian background, Kukkula School*)

What is also noteworthy in this division is that it roughly followed the ethnic divisions within the school. One of the original schools had been mostly white and Finnish, while the other had been more ethnically mixed – thus the merging decision can be seen as related to the 'mixing' policies that are widely used to prevent segregation both in education and housing policy in the Helsinki metropolitan area. This difference was, even at the time of the interviews, reflected in the two groupings so that one consisted

4 Similar decisions had been made in many comprehensive schools in Helsinki within the previous years. According to Official Statistics of Finland (2019), the number of comprehensive schools in Helsinki had decreased by over 20 schools since year 2010. The trend is similar in Finland as a whole (ibid.).

of only white, and mostly Finnish, boys, whereas the other was ethnically mixed.

**In Harju School**, participants were recruited from the sixth grade and were all 12-year-olds. As in the first school (Nurmi), the organisation of the school buildings reflected the old division between primary and lower secondary schools. The division between primary and lower secondary schools was internalised by the pupils, who were sixth-graders, the oldest in the school, and therefore also the most well-known pupils and 'the bosses' in the school. The sixth-graders were considered to be at the top of the hierarchy because of their seniority and proximity to the lower secondary school ('like outta school already'). While the older pupils in the upper grades were seen as being even higher up the hierarchy, they were not considered part of the (sub)hierarchy of the primary school pupils, since their world was separate and they were not interested in the pupils in the lower grades. There had been no great changes in the composition of classes – all except one of the interviewees had studied in the school for several years – and the social order in the school appeared to be well established (although not fixed).

Harju School offered all the pupils the possibility to choose specialist sports classes (among other options) – an offer that all participants in the focus group discussion had taken up. Engaging in sports was very important in terms of masculine hierarchies and social groupings: the boys in the school were constructed as divided either into sporty boys or gamer boys. Sporty boys were the bigger group and sportiness was connected to greater popularity in the school. The interviewees particularly liked the sports classes, but they also described their school as nice and calm more generally, contrasting it with some other schools where, according to them, bullying was more common and more severe.

MP: What do you think of the school in general, that is how does it…?

Olli: Quite nice.

Luka: Yea it is quite nice.

Bikram: There are great guys here.

Luka: You make friends easily here and—

Bikram: In other schools… And there is quite a lot of bullying in other schools as there is not that much bullying here.

Luka: This is, like quite a peaceful place in that way. (…)

Mikael: [In other schools, according to what friends have said] [T]hey call you names, and push you around, and do all kinds of such things.

Bikram: I have a friend who said, well who told me that he/she had heard that, somebody got their head dipped in a toilet.

MP: Okay well that sounds nasty.

Bikram: Yeah it is a bit wilder.

Mikael: Like in some movie.

MP: But here it is, calmer?

Bikram: It is calm here.

Luka: It is calm here yeah.

Bikram: And severe teachers so nobody dares to. (*Focus group 6, 5 boys, 12 years, one Finnish, two with migrant parents, two mixed parentage, Harju School*)

Here too, then, violence is one of the themes through which the boys describe the school's atmosphere, even though this is done by differentiating between one's own school and allegedly more violent schools. This school was located in the least affluent residential area of the three, and the inhabitants and schools in such areas often have to face stigmatising assumptions concerning their area and school. The boys' narrative on the school's positive ambiance may thus be also read in the context of what has been written about the discursive strategies of pupils studying in 'disadvantaged' schools: that it is often important for them to locate the assumed problems elsewhere and construct the school as 'good (enough)' (e.g. Reay, 2007).

## Boys (and Girls) in School

Since the chapters that follow focus more on content than context, here we wish briefly to discuss how the participants positioned themselves in relation to school and how masculinities were present in narratives about the school context. Boys' relationships with school have repeatedly been a cause for concern in Finnish public discussion on boys and masculinities (Arnesen et al., 2008; Vettenranta et al., 2016). Many boys in the study explained that school was important for them, that they wanted to do well in order to succeed in further studies and life more generally, and that they made effort with their schoolwork. However, they also produced well-worn stories of girls being hard-working and meticulous, while boys were freedom-loving, worked less hard, but were possibly more talented than girls. For instance, in a focus group discussion of five boys, individual differences in learning were recognised and all the boys reported valuing success in school and getting good grades. However, (some) girls were represented as putting '100 per cent effort' into schoolwork, sometimes succeeding very well and getting the best grades but sometimes not succeeding despite their efforts. In contrast, Onni described himself as someone who gets good grades without much effort, and Eino, who said that he was revising for exams, emphasised the strategic nature and relaxedness of his revision work in contrast to girls:

Onni: Among girls [in the class] there is that one person who everyone probably recognises, who actually puts a *terrible* lot of effort in school and wants to get the ten [the best grade] from all subjects. (…) Who puts 100% effort into school. (…) Of course I'm not saying that I wouldn't put effort into school, but anyway, I have time for other things as well than school.

MP: Is it the kind of thing more in general in your opinion that girls put more effort into school than boys?

Lauri: Well it depends a bit. In our class all of the girls now are, I don't know if they put effort, I guess they do but… so there's many–

Martin: [Who] are always late.

Lauri: Many, like they, in a way it's good if they even pass the year. [laughs]

Onni: Yeah there are the kind who clearly try but they simply can't do it, so for them school is difficult.

MP: Like for the girls?

Onni: Yeah, and in boys there is that too for sure. I have said myself that I think I'm quite good in school but like, I don't in the end probably study a lot for the exams but I still get nines and nine and a halves and like that. So the things stick in my head very well.

Eino: At least I, I mean, well I don't know, I'm as well quite like average so I don't in the end put a lot of effort into school, but like, into all the exams and like that I start to revise quite in time. Because of that my mum has given such good reasons why you should start to revise so early and then because it's quite nice because you can revise like in a relaxed way that you can for example read one chapter per day and then, in a way you don't have to read the whole day. (*Focus group 5, 5 boys, 14–15 years, four Finnish, one with migrant parents, Kukkula School*)

Working hard for school and caring a lot about grades were particularly seen as more typical of girls than boys, and a boy who put too much effort into schoolwork was seen as not properly masculine. Being seen as caring too much about school lowered a boy's position in the masculine hierarchy and also made him a potential target for teasing and bullying. For instance, Daniel (12 years, mixed parentage) said that what is offensive for boys is calling them 'wimps or nerds', and he later defined a nerd as someone who 'doesn't really focus on anything else than computers or the school'. These were characteristics the boys wanted to distance themselves from.

The gendered difference in (being seen as) putting effort into schoolwork was even more clearly stated in a focus group discussion with a girl and a trans boy, who also produced discourses of girls as hard-working and boys as underachieving to point out that it is only fair that girls' school work is recognised, for instance, in scholarships awards:

> Katriina: And then in my opinion, more a girl thing, or is thought so, is clearly school and studying. Like, even our teacher suggested that there should be scholarships, like for school performing, so that in every class one for boys and one for girls so that also the boys would get one. And I was a bit like now is that fair? [laughs]
>
> Sami: Or like, many girls have been working just ridiculously hard and so they concentrate in the class, are not on their phone, do their homework, they study for the exams.
>
> Katriina: Yes like I have one friend who gets some five hours a night sleep because she studies so much.
>
> Sami: Yes then it would be very unfair if she didn't get the scholarship because some boy who has an average value 7,8 gets it, who is all the time on phone, just because he's a boy and he needs a chance. Or, like, there are the kind of specificities that, I can say that boys are sometimes considered a bit worse in the school system and then they have the exclusion problem when they don't succeed in school, and they're a bit more immature so that it's a bit more difficult to get along at school. But it doesn't mean that if we and some girls work hard so then everything should be taken away from them. (*Focus group 7, a girl and a trans boy, 15 years, Finnish background, Keinu youth club*)

As discussed above, most of the interviewees described their schools as 'good schools', regardless of the social class differences in the schools' reputations based on their locations in socio-economically different residential areas. They also generally gave positive descriptions of their teachers. Individual teachers were described as being able to make a big difference to what the participants thought about their schoolwork: many of the boys pointed out that a 'nice teacher' made it enjoyable to study even those subjects that they otherwise disliked or found difficult. However, boys considered some teacher practices unfair. The theme that was mentioned in all schools and all focus groups was that some teachers tended to consider boys 'the usual suspects' when it came to misbehaviour in the classroom. This resulted, according to the boys, in the teachers interacting in a more positive way with girls and ignoring their misbehaviour, while 'yelling' at and disciplining the boys.

> MP: So do you think that the teachers, do they treat boys and girls in the same way or is there a difference there?
>
> Bikram: Most of the teachers yea but then for example our music teacher, she, like, works more with the girls. And our teacher too more with the girls somehow. [But] all the boys have noticed that yet the girls have not noticed anything.
>
> MP: Is it so that they ask more questions from the girls or that somehow…?
>
> Bikram: They do not yell that much to them and so on.
>
> MP: Oh even thought they would have been causing ruckus or?
>
> Bikram: Yea like this once I was doing, as it was an exam day and I wasn't there that day so I had to do the exam on another day, so every time my friends laughed they got yelled at, as the girls giggled all the time well it was kinda… Them, the teacher told them that if they wanted to talk well go to the hall, but to boys for example she only said be quiet and so on.
>
> MP: So some things feel kinda unfair?
>
> Bikram: Yea unfair. But I didn't think that she tries that much, she can be quite fair but sometimes it does not work. (*Individual interview Bikram, 12 years, Nepalese background, Harju School*)

That teachers sometimes disciplined boys for behaviour they ignored in girls was partly recognised by the girl participants, too, although Vilja points out that this may be due to the gendered differences in frequency of misbehaviour in boys and in girls:

> Vilja: Sure, girls may behave badly too, like, all teens may behave badly but like, it may be about that the certain boys have behaved badly for a long time already, so the teacher explodes to them easier than to someone else who does the same thing but like, for the first time. (*Individual interview Vilja, 15 years, Finnish background*)

The participants generally appreciated teachers they considered fair. Other important characteristics of good teachers were said to be calmness, friendliness, and the ability to negotiate and investigate what has happened, as well as strictness and caring for pupils' learning.

> Onni: [A good teacher is] Strict enough, not like the kind [of teacher] who allows you to do whatever you want. Also like that they are calm, that they aren't instantly if something happens that someone does [something] wrong or is being stupid in class, so they aren't instantly aggressive [when they] take it up, but tries calmly to handle the issue. And then the kind that if you ask help from them then they actually help, and not just in principle a bit like supposedly help, but then you can't get anything out of it anyway. (*Focus group 5, 5 boys, 14–15 years, four with Finnish background, one with migrant parents, Kukkula School*)

The desire for the teachers to be strict (enough) was repeated in several interviews and appears to contradict the masculine norm of not caring too much about school. For instance, Lauri made a distinction between 'terribly strict' teachers who confiscated pupils' mobile phones to ensure their concentration and those teachers who made concentrating entirely a pupil's own responsibility. When asked which he preferred, Lauri did not hesitate to say confiscation.

> Lauri: Yes they're quite, some are like in a way terribly strict that you can't be on the phone which is now quite a self-evident but they might take it away. And then some in a way put it to your own, or to my responsibility that I would use the phone so I don't then focus in the class and learn them.

MP: Yes that it's your own responsibility then?

Lauri: Yes.

MP: Which way is so-called better, that—?

Lauri: Probably that the phone is taken away entirely. (*Individual interview Lauri, 14 years, Finnish background, Kukkula School*)

Given that masculine norms are not necessarily easily reconciled with school norms, it may be a lesser risk for a boy's position in masculine hierarchies if a teacher *makes* them follow the school rule than if they follow the school rule on their own initiative. The strictness of teachers was, however, also described as good because it prevented bullying in school. However, one interviewee considered the strictness of one particular teacher – when it manifested in aggressive 'yelling' – as frightening and having negative countereffects:

> Our teacher like, in my opinion, yells quite a lot. A bit too much I think. (…) [A good teacher] explains to a small [child], smaller than s/he is that that was a bad thing and if one does too many bad thing then s/he may yell. But not immediately, so that the child just, he doesn't know why she is yelling and so he does even more bad things. (*Individual interview Ivan, 12 years, Russian background, Harju School*)

## Leisure Time and Hobbies

Outside schools, leisure time and extra-curricular activities ('hobbies') were important contexts that were much discussed in the interviews. Negotiation of masculinities takes place in all the young people's everyday environments, and, while school is certainly a central context for these negotiations, so too are leisure spaces. Hobbies are an important part of leisure time for Finnish young people in this age group (e.g. Hakanen, Myllyniemi and Salasuo, 2018) and, for many, questions about leisure time evoked reflections on particular organised activities. Hobbies were often referred to when the participants first introduced themselves at the beginning of the interview, along with name, age and grade, when Marja asked the interviewees 'to tell something about themselves'. For many, talking about hobbies was an enjoyable theme with which to start the interview, since it was concrete and allowed the interviewees to talk about something they were knowledgeable about that was safely masculine and shared with most other young people.

Of the 32 interviewees, only four reported that they did not currently engage in any organised extra-curricular activity, one of them having given up his earlier sports hobby reluctantly and temporarily because of a recently diagnosed disease. As has been reported in a survey on Finnish young people's leisure activities (Hakanen, Myllyniemi and Salasuo, 2018), young people do not necessarily perceive their self-initiated, independent interests (rather than organised classes) as 'hobbies', even though they may invest heavily in them. In these data, too, the participants described several interests that they engaged in independently during their leisure time, such as photography, coding, image processing, history, drawing, music and graffiti, but these were rarely called 'hobbies'. Similarly, playing computer/video games was described as a pleasant and common leisure time activity, but this was not considered 'a hobby' – perhaps due to the contradiction between the pleasure that gaming gave to the participants and its perception as a potentially harmful activity in the eyes of the participants' parents and other adults around them (see Chapter 5). On the other hand, independent sports activities like skateboarding, cycling, bodyweight training and riding a kick-scooter were called hobbies.

By and large, then, for the interviewees 'hobbies' were organised activities, which were most commonly related to sports, and football in particular. Of the 28 interviewees who identified as boys, 19 were engaged with at least one sports hobby. Ten played football (soccer). Other organised sports hobbies mentioned were basketball, tennis, parkour, ice hockey, boxing and jujutsu. Four boys said they played an instrument, and some reported hobbies like scouting and ping-pong. This fits with findings from surveys of young people, which find that sports are a common hobby for young people (regardless of gender) and, among boys in this age group, football is the most popular sports hobby, followed by other team sports (Hakanen, Myllyniemi and Salasuo, 2018: 32; Myllyniemi and Berg, 2013). This also fits with the recurrent finding in masculinity studies that physicality and prowess in sports are seen as 'masculine' qualities, and in many environments constitute part of hegemonic masculinities. While boys benefit from being good at sport in terms of their position in masculine hierarchies, the Finnish Child Victim Survey also shows that boys experience more violence than girls in organised sports (and other organised activities). This suggests that these environments contribute to socialising boys into masculine norms where aggression and violence are normalised (Peltola and Kivijärvi, 2017). Football in particular has been found to be an important social arena for 'doing boy' and excluding girls (e.g. Frosh et al., 2002; Swain, 2000; Yang, 2020). In this study, football was not only reported to be an important hobby for several boys but was also a central form of masculine sociability in Harju School particularly. It was an important part of informal leisure time activities (such as 'hanging out').

The four girls who participated in interviews also reported that they participated in a variety of organised and self-initiated hobbies, including football, music, theatre, drawing, circus and writing – activities that are fairly common in Finland.

Organised activities play an important role in youth politics in Finland, as they are generally considered 'safe' and 'educational' forms of leisure activity (Peltola and Kivijärvi, 2017). There is, for instance, a political initiative called the 'Hobby Guarantee' that seeks to find a way of offering all children and young people the opportunity to participate in at least one organised activity, regardless of their families' socio-economic status. This is an attempt to answer the challenge of the increasing costs of young people's organised activities and thus increasing social inequalities in accessing them (e.g. Puronaho, 2014). In this study, almost all participants reported having at least one hobby, and thus organised activities were available for participants living in different residential areas and from different social class backgrounds. However, in the affluent Nurmi School the participants reported several hobbies and named more exclusive activities (e.g. golf, aerial acrobatics) than the participants in the two other schools. Some of the participants in Nurmi School also talked about their leisure time as filled with several activities, which left no time for everything that they wished to do. In all other research locations (Kukkula and Harju Schools; Keinu Youth Club), there were individual participants whose families were less affluent, who reported having or having had hard times economically. Two of them explained that economic hardships had reduced their opportunities to engage in organised activities. However, that most participants in less affluent families did engage with hobbies they liked probably reflects both that such activities are considered part of the norms of 'good parenthood' (Berg and Peltola, 2015) and that offering enjoyable leisure activities to children is prioritised even by parents who are struggling economically.

CHAPTER 3

# Hegemonic Masculinities and Constructions of Gender Differences

The concept of 'hegemonic masculinity' is ubiquitous in research on masculinities. As detailed in Chapter 1, it is an idealised representation that is considered to organise boys' and men's practices in that it is both the most powerful version of masculinity and normatively prescribed (del Aguila, 2013). It has, however, been much critiqued, partly because it often elides the process of formation of masculinity as a gendered social category and different kinds of masculinity (Hearn et al., 2014) and partly because there are multiple ways in which men are powerful. There are, therefore, hegemonic masculinities, in the plural. Hearn et al. (2014) suggested that the focus should be on the hegemony of actual men and boys rather than hegemonic masculinities in general and that these should be examined transnationally and intersectionally.

In research on boys, the features generally identified as characterising hegemonic masculinities entail (threats of) violence, toughness, fighting, sporting prowess, homophobia, joking relationships and popularity (Frosh et al., 2002; Manninen et al., 2011). While boys differ in relation to these characteristics and more 'inclusive' versions of masculinity have been identified (Anderson, 2018), this constellation of characteristics patterns their everyday practices. Yet, as Connell and Messerschmidt

(2005) and Messerschmidt (2019) suggest, few boys embody hegemonic masculinity and thus it is largely aspirational, rather than a lived reality. Further, studies by Renold (2004) and Way and colleagues (2014) have shown that many boys feel powerless or anxious about the impossibility of attaining masculine norms and are critical of the characteristics connected with hegemonic masculinities, even though they may remain complicit with them in their everyday interactions. Schools constitute a fruitful site for the study of hegemonic masculinities in that the space of school means that different kinds of young people are 'thrown together' (Massey, 2005). For that reason, boys need to negotiate how they 'do' boy in processes of being and becoming masculine that involve belonging, investment in, or rejection of, peer cultures in particular institutions (Ward and Thurnell-Read, 2019).

The issues raised by a consideration of hegemonic masculinities are extensive and will be addressed across several chapters. However, this chapter begins the process of interrogating the concept. This chapter examines how both equality discourses and essentialised gender differences are present in participants' talk about gender and examines the ways in which boys differentiate themselves from girls. This differentiation was a pervasive and marked feature of the boys' narratives in both group discussions and individual interviews and was reiterated in response to questions about a range of topics.

Overall, the findings suggest that boys do not simply reproduce old narratives about gender. In keeping with research that suggests that masculinities are changing, the boys produced themes that are both contemporary and consonant with gender norms in Finnish society. They maintained that girls and boys are equal and were critical of notions that, for example, boys should not cry. Yet, many of their narratives simultaneously constructed a gendered hierarchy in which boys are superior to girls and some masculinities are preferable to others. The holding of these apparently contradictory narratives indicates that there is social and generational change in gendered beliefs, but that everyday practices and imagining of contemporary and future gender practices are highly differentiated.

## Gender Equality Discourses

As discussed in Chapter 1, Finland prides itself on gender equality. Despite evidence that gender inequalities remain both in the labour market and in the private sphere (e.g. Julkunen, 2010), discourses of gender equality, such as those emphasising equal opportunities, are a strong, even normative part of the Finnish national narrative. It comes, therefore, as no surprise that the participants, regardless of gender, embraced these gender equality discourses. In their narratives, equal rights across genders, together with notions that gender 'makes no difference' or that individual interests and differences override any gender differences, were among the elements through which genders were constructed as equal. These discourses were prominent especially in those (often early) parts of the interviews where gender was discussed at an abstract, general level detached from the participants' everyday lives.

In a focus group discussion with five boys in Harju School, gender differences were discussed as follows:

> MP: What do you think, is it different to be a boy than a girl?
>
> Mikael: It is a bit.
>
> Bikram: It is different but everyone has the same rights and such.
>
> Mikael: Well like for example what your interests are.
>
> Luka: It is not like if you were a boy you have more– [rights]
>
> Bikram: You could do this–
>
> Luka: So that you could do this or, you could do that and if one were a girl then for example you cannot do some other thing, but really everyone can do the same things.
>
> Mikael: But then again they might not be interested in the same things as boys.
>
> Luka: Yea.
>
> Bikram: But some are interested. (*Focus group 6, 5 boys, 12 years, one with Finnish, two with migrant parents, two mixed parentage, Harju School*)

The boys agreed that being a boy is 'a bit different' to being a girl, but the difference stems from different interests rather than different rights. Luka stated specifically that boys do not have 'more rights', that gender does not define what one 'could do' and that 'everyone can do the same things'. Mikael nuanced this understanding by pointing out that interests may differ according to gender – which explains and justifies the (slight) difference between girls and boys. This is agreed with by Luka but further nuanced by Bikram, who points out that there may still be girls who are interested in the same things as boys. What is worth noticing is the very abstract level of discussion, typical of gender equality discourses in the data. No concrete examples are mentioned either concerning the things girls or boys 'can do' or concerning their allegedly different interests.

Johannes from Nurmi School started his reflection on whether there are things that 'only boys do' with an observation from his everyday life on boys playing more video games, especially the football game *FIFA*, but quickly went on to point out exceptions and then to indicate repeatedly that there are really no differences between girls and boys, except for the biological differences:

MP: Are there those kinds of things that you do only with a boy group or that only boys do?

Johannes: Well I'm not saying that the girls wouldn't play [video games] but, maybe usually the boys play more. They do exist in the world, I know many girls who play. (…) Nowadays there isn't actually any terrible, that, girls and boys, separation in, what you like. It's more, just that… [break 6 s]. Actually there isn't anything, that girls would do different things from boys. Quite a lot even play FIFA, or a couple. (…) It is hard to say. Like even girls play quite a bit. There is not so much any, difference.

MP: What if there were for example an alien exploring the globe and you should explain it what a boy is, then could you explain it?

Johannes: Well I wouldn't know, today it's just, more like, the differences are maybe biological only. Yes in fact it is that there's none actually.

MP: Then otherwise, people are all their own way?

Johannes: Yeah.

MP: You already said that you spend time with, or that you also have girls as friends.

Johannes: Yes. There's nothing [special about it]. (…)

MP: Have you ever thought that, some things would be easier for girls or, easier for boys?

Johannes: No, not as such in any way. There isn't really anything that would be easier or harder. There's not really, that you would think of the difference anymore, like, it was in the kindergarten like 'girl germs'! [laughs] There is nothing special. (*Individual interview Johannes, 13 years, Finnish background, Nurmi School*)

Johannes referred several times to gender differences being non-existent or insignificant *nowadays* or *today*. Towards the end of the extract, this temporal dimension is concretised when Johannes compares and contrasts his current understanding of gender differences with the allegedly more pronounced gender boundaries in the nursery school. His laughter marks the latter as inferior or childish understanding, and thus his current way of representing gender differences as minimal constructs him within the more mature position he claims (in other parts of the interview as well).

Valtteri, also from Nurmi School, approached the same question – whether there are things that only girls or boys do – from a different angle but also in a way that renders gender differences insignificant:

MP: What do you think that are there like, things that only girls do and only boys do, is there something like that, can you think of anything?

Valtteri: Of course there aren't those kind of things that only either one does because, nowadays there are all sorts of weird people, who can have like for example chair as their gender. So that, there aren't any things either that only chairs do, like some other person can do those same things as chairs.

MP: What do you think about if someone says their gender is a chair?

Valtteri: I think it's a bit like, I haven't met that many chairs but, it's okay. (*Focus group 4, 2 boys, 12 years, Finnish background, Nurmi School*)

In explaining why gender does not define people's interests, Valtteri built on the idea of different and non-binary gender identities by referring to people who consider themselves neither boys nor girls but – humorously – chairs. The idea that, since gender is fluid, it cannot define people's interests or actions explains Valtteri's initial response, 'of course there aren't'. While his point on gender fluidity and non-binary gender identities may appear to be part of an egalitarian discourse, it is noteworthy that Valtteri simultaneously distanced himself from people with non-binary gender identities by the choice of the word ('chair') that in its absurdity verges on ridiculing people with non-binary gender identities as well as by calling such people 'weird'.

In the examples above, boys gave a 'different, but equal' discourse, pointing out that what differentiates boys and girls are their interests and pastimes, even though Johannes veered between saying the differences are biological to saying there are 'none actually'. The extract from the discussion with Valtteri shows that the contemporary discussions on gender and its complexity may very well be known to the young people, even if shifting understandings of gender may also produce discomfort.

Gender equality discourses, especially those emphasising similar opportunities (even if there is research evidence to the contrary), are thus very familiar and even normative ways for young people in this age group to discuss gender. However, these discourses do not necessarily connect with actual people and events in the participants' everyday lives. Indeed, egalitarian discourses such as those above were generally contradicted by the ways in which boys also produced narratives of essentialised gender differences.

## Essentialising Gendered Differences

The following extract from a focus group with four boys illuminates how boys 'do' masculinities through joking relationships. They essentialise gender differences and at the same time establish their superiority over girls.

> MP: Okay. Are boys and girls the same?
>
> Elmeri: No, we are better in everything.
>
> Jaakko: There's more water in us yeah. [Daniel: Yeah.]
>
> MP: You are better in everything?
>
> Daniel: There's more water in us.
>
> MP: You have more water, yeah, what else?
>
> Daniel: Boys have a magic wand. [laughter]
>
> Jaakko: Why did you have to use the name magic wand? (…)
>
> MP: Right. Well you said that you are better than girls in everything? [laughs]
>
> Elmeri: Well like, to be sure, we are better in sports, then we are better leaders, we have a better sense of coordination. So we are better in quite many things now. (…)
>
> MP: Well how about girls then, are they interested somehow in different things or?
>
> Daniel: They are quite a lot.
>
> Elmeri: Well yeah, quite a lot. In magic wands. [laughing] (*Focus group 3, 4 boys, 13 years, three with Finnish background, one mixed parentage, Nurmi School*)

The above extract is noteworthy in many ways, not least because, coming at the start of the focus group, the boys wrong-footed the interviewer by giving an answer she did not expect and, since she is a woman, setting themselves up as better than her. The first response, 'No, we are better in everything', may be unsettling, but the following response, 'There's more water in us', which is repeated by Daniel, is puzzling and leaves Marja's questions trailing as the boys co-construct a narrative of being better than girls, initially only explaining that they have 'more water' in them. When, having repeated this, Marja asked for elaboration, Daniel alluded to penises in a way that defended against censure from the woman interviewer because it was cloaked in apparent innocence. At the same time, the statement 'Boys have a magic wand' opened the way for all the boys to laugh uproariously, doing hegemonic masculinity through joking, quick repartee and showing that they could make and laugh at jokes as insiders. For Marja, as the researcher, this exclusionary joking signalled a dead end and she returned to the initial statement: 'Right. Well you said that you are better than girls in everything?' turning it into a question and laughing. It is at this point that it becomes apparent that, while the boys have not taken the interview seriously until now, Elmeri, who gave the first response, had a well-worn account of how boys are better than girls. His three-part list of sports, leadership and coordination are elements that can be understood as part of hegemonic masculinity. When Marja shifted the focus to girls, Elmeri steered the conversation back to magic wands – this time suggesting that girls desire them.

As pubescent boys, the allusive focus on boys' sexual organs allowed the boys to perform hierarchical, hegemonic and heterosexual masculinity, drawing on biology to construct their narrative. It is an example of how the boys were able to construct essentialist gender differences in exclusionary ways, in this case excluding the woman interviewer but implicitly excluding girls in general. From this perspective, the boys were clearly not interested in claiming or doing inclusive masculinity (which is neither homophobic nor hegemonic) (Anderson and McCormack, 2018). Extracts such as those above highlight the importance of an intersectional perspective that takes forward Connell's (1995) recognition that masculinity is built on relations between boys and men and girls and women.

The essentialising of gender differences partly comes from seeing boys' and girls' activities and choices as gender-segregated, which was a recurrent theme in boys' and girls' accounts. In the following extract Mikael talks of differences between girls and boys based on his experiences both at school and at home with his sister.

MP: Are you [boys] different from girls?

Mikael: Yeah, quite, I don't know – quite a lot.

MP: In what sort of things?

Mikael: Maybe, for example during the breaks we do sports much more, they may only stand and talk and like this. Then, maybe, the way to dress, even in winters and in general, usually boys have more clothes on.

MP: Girls have somehow, thinner or, less clothes?

Mikael: Less clothes, usually. Even my big sister, when she, I remember well when she started like at the 6th grade, no more outer pants. But then, we boys we may put. (…)

MP: So but what was your sister thinking, did she think it was somehow embarrassing or why she didn't want them anymore?

Mikael: When her friends didn't use them anymore, so then she didn't want to use them either.

MP: Do things like that affect boys as well, like if friends are wearing certain kinds of clothes then, or is it more like a girls' thing?

Mikael: Girls' thing. Yes we may, we don't, we never mock if someone puts something on. Usually we just say, like 'those are cool and I want those too' and something. (*Individual interview Mikael, 12 years, mixed parentage, Harju School*)

When asked whether boys are different from girls, Mikael started tentatively ('yeah, quite, I don't know – quite a lot') but went on to itemise differences in terms of sport, clothing and being influenced by friends that fit with his group interview extract above. Girls are constructed in his account as less active than boys, less sensibly dressed and less independent of their friends' opinions. Unlike in the extract above, where the boys explicitly said that boys are better than girls in everything, Mikael did not explicitly make this claim. Yet, his narrative has the same effect, constructing girls as inferior to boys. It is not a 'different, but equal' narrative.

It is noteworthy that, for Mikael, gendered cultural practices at home and school leaked into each other. He drew on what he knew about his sister to help him to understand girls at school and to explain gendered difference. Having a sister is, therefore, important since boys and girls remain unfamiliar with each other at school at this age. Despite his limited familiarity with girls, Mikael's account fits with gendered time use studies in that boys and girls are found to do markedly different things in various countries, including Finland (Gracia et al., 2020).

It might be expected that since boys seem to take for granted what seem like fixed, stereotypic differences, that they would not be concerned about being treated in essentialist ways. This is not, however, the case. Boys considered it an area of social injustice that girls have more freedom to do 'boyish' things than boys to do 'girlish' things. This is exemplified in first Martin's individual interview and then a discussion with two younger boys, Kristian and Valtteri.

Martin: Like, boys cannot have an emotio—, they cannot cry for example or something since they are, boys, and something like that. So when for example a girl does something boyish, she is applauded for it but when a boy does something girlish, he is laughed at. So, they want girls to have more options than boys.

MP: So it actually feels like girls are allowed to do more, different things and boys not really.

Martin: Yea.

MP: What are the girlish things a boy can do to get laughed at for?

Martin: For example learning to dance or something, cheerleading. (*Individual interview Martin, 15 years, Estonian background, Kukkula School*)

MP: Do they bully girls and boys for the same things?

Valtteri: No, because, boys, for example if some girl buys from a shop My Little Pony things then she's not bullied, but if a boy goes and does the same then, he's bullied, probably. And like if some of our classmates saw me buying My Little Pony things then they would probably laugh quite a lot.

MP: What were you about to say?

Kristian: Yeah you could have compared it to that if some girl buys exactly those, fighting games but one can't be bullied for that. That would just be for some of them, ordinary dumb girls a bit strange that she would buy some weird girl stuff.

Valtteri: Yeah, they wouldn't be bullied, that, they [girls] don't bully [you] so easily no matter what you did but like, boys bully a bit more easily in my opinion than, girls, for easier things and, like that.

Kristian: I never bully.

Valtteri: I don't either but like, for example if a boy does something not-boyish.

MP: Yeah is it like this My Little Pony thing for example?

Valtteri: Yeah, then they will be bullied quite easily or, for example if a boy makes a mistake in something then everyone just laughs at him, all the other boys but, if a girl makes a mistake in something then everyone is just like good, and you will know next time and like that support her, more. (*Focus group 4, 2 boys, 12 years, Finnish background, Nurmi School*)

Martin picked out the showing of emotion as a difference in what boys and girls are allowed to do. Boys are not allowed to cry (an expectation that some other boys also spontaneously raised as unfair) and girls are applauded for doing 'boyish' things, whereas boys are laughed at for doing 'something girlish' like learning to dance or cheerleading. It is noteworthy that Martin was systematically vague about who is unfair in this way. Indeed, in his evaluative statement, 'So, *they* want girls to have more options than boys', it never becomes clear who 'they' are. In Valtteri's and Kristian's discussion, the difference in treatment of 'cross-gender' behaviour is that boys are laughed at and bullied for doing 'girlish' things, while girls are not. Both Martin and Valtteri and Kristian referred to being laughed at as a significant social sanction; it may be that being laughed at constitutes bullying since, although joking relations are central to hegemonic masculinities, being laughed at runs counter to this. In Valtteri's and Kristian's view, girls are more accepting of girls making mistakes than boys are of boys doing so, which seems to contradict the notion (propounded by Mikael above) that girls just do what other girls do, presumably because they are afraid to do otherwise – although, of course, it is common for people to hold contradictory practices and beliefs.

From both these extracts, it is possible to see potential dynamism in gendered relations and practices in that the three boys in the extracts see this gender difference as unfair and illegitimate. This is important but should not be seen as something qualitatively 'new' in masculinity constructions, since it has long been pointed out that it is more acceptable for girls to act like boys since boys are higher status, but not vice-versa (Frosh et al., 2002). Adler, Kless and Adler (1992) reported similar findings three decades ago.

> To a greater extent than did the boys, then, they attained some gender-role expansion: They could more acceptably pursue the traditionally male avenues of sports, achievement, autonomy, and initiative toward the opposite sex. Such a cross-over among boys into 'feminine' areas was less acceptable, however, and still negatively sanctioned. (Adler, Kless and Adler, 1992: 185)

In the next extract, from Nurmi School, Marja sought to establish whether boys have become more egalitarian than previous generations by asking how they see gender differences and, if so, how.

> MP: Right. How about then if you think about these things like, well are there some things that girls can't do because they're

girls and boys can't do because they are boys? Or don't want to? (…)

Leo: At this age at least boys don't usually wear make-up. That is at least at this age still, a girls' thing. And… Yeah. And then after all when all the hobbies are divided into so many parts (…)

Sofia: And then there is that if some boys start to wear make-up, because it's classified as a girls' thing then they can start to call him names so-called gay and like that. So like, that's quite a bad thing.

MP: Does something come to mind that what could be what…?

Elsa: A girl is thought to be weird if she for example, fights. [laughs] Or like that rare you see girls fighting in the school corridors unlike when boys always fight in the school corridors.

MP: Do boys fight a lot here in the school corridors?…

Veeti: Well it's a bit like– kind of playful, so that you like to take [wrestler's] holds and wrestle and so on. Probably exactly, those kind of cool throws of the films and some these type of [laughing] locks. (*Focus group 2, 2 boys and 2 girls, 12–13 years, Finnish background, Nurmi School*)

This extract reiterates findings from many contemporary studies in countries including South Africa (Tucker and Govender, 2017), Bulgaria, Italy, Latvia, Slovenia, the UK (Gough, Milnes and Turner-Moore, 2019) and the USA (Levesque, 2016) that boys seek to establish clear differences from girls. The above focus group is evenly gender balanced, with two girls and two boys, all of whom spoke in the short extract. While Leo, a boy, immediately replied to Marja's question about whether girls and boys do different things by explaining that boys do not wear make-up and the hobbies are different, Sofia opened issues of power relations and homophobic name-calling by pointing out that, if some boys start to wear make-up, they can be called gay, something she took a stand against, saying 'So like, that's quite a bad thing'. This seems to be a conversation stopper so Marja asked if anything else comes to mind, at which point Elsa shifted attention to what would be thought 'weird' for girls to do, fighting in the school corridors, doing so in a light-hearted way. This then gave Veeti an entry point to explain both that this boys' behaviour is playful and skilled and to link it with 'cool' popular culture.

The point here is that, whether Marja asked whether girls and boys are the same, or about their activities, the boys and girls agreed that there are socially marked differences between them and that breaching the socially constructed gender divides can be costly for young people because of the power relations involved. In the above extract, unlike the first one, no one suggested that boys or girls are hierarchically superior to each other. However, there is a hint that boys who engage in behaviour seen as girlish can suffer penalties that, as we shall see below, fit with notions that masculinities continue to be linked with homophobia and heteronormativity (Hall, 2020).

## Boys' Relations with Girls

The above discussion has shown that a pervasive finding from the study is that the young people view boys and girls as different and that boys tend to see girls as inferior in various ways. While they indicate that these differences result from interest in different activities and different relations with peers, it is not clear why those differences result in the degree of social segregation the young people report and that was evident in informal observations in the study schools. The following three extracts below, from the same focus group, illuminate why boys feel that the different cultures of girls and boys lead to a lack of familiarity with each other in this age group.

MP: Well how about, how about in your class so do girls and boys hang out together or is it more like that girls amongst each other and boys amongst each other?

Onni: Quite like that [separately], rarely like… [together]

MP: Separately.

Martin: When you must.

Onni: Yeah it feels a bit like that, well I don't know what the girls think, but I feel a bit that they like isolate themselves. So for me it wouldn't matter in principle if there were girls or not, but it feels like girls isolate [themselves] into their own group. So, okay from other classes there are girls and boys in the same, but from our class none at all in fact. (…) And I have actually, I always try to start a conversation but then you either hear a sneer or nothing. So that is a bit difficult to chat there because you don't have the other participant.

MP: Okay yeah right. What could it be about?

Onni: I don't know if they're shy.

Lauri: Probably about friend groups. [laughs]

Onni: I don't know, maybe… no idea. (*Focus group 5, 5 boys, 14–15 years, four with Finnish background, one with migrant parents, Kukkula School*)

In answer to Marja's question, Onni agreed that boys and girls are generally separate. Martin's interjection 'When you must' seems to suggest that boys are reluctant to have to spend time with girls. However, this runs counter to what Onni went on to say. According to Onni, girls choose to self-isolate and, indeed, either sneer or ignore him when he tries to start conversations with them. His account made girls' behaviour out to be both rude and inexplicable (although he says that he does not know if they are shy) as well as holding them responsible for gender segregation while entirely exonerating boys. The discussion then went on:

MP: Right. Well if you think about what things, or let's continue from here so what things do boys do and are they somehow different from what girls do, so are there some things that a boy can't ever do? Some things what girls would do but boys can't do?

Martin: Well I can't go to the toilet together with my friends because it looks weird. [joint laughter]

MP: Okay well that is a good, concrete example.

Onni: It is exactly, I have at times always asked for example from some friend of mine that why do girls go at the same time to the toilet, but they don't really know how to answer that either. I don't know what's the reason for that, but like. Then again if boys go to the bathroom at the same time then it feels that there is something.

Martin: Something [has] happened.

Onni: Yeah something actually bad or different is happening, but then again if girls go then no one is interested really.

Lauri: Yeah and then they squeeze into the same toilet stall.

Onni: Yeah we have a joke about that, that are they making some chair there or something, so what happens there. [joint laughter]

MP: Okay, yeah yeah. Does someone have some other example of what girls do but boys don't?

Eino: Well at least I don't know that any boy would ride horses. (*Focus group 5, 5 boys, 14–15 years, four with Finnish background, one with migrant parents, Kukkula School*)

Here, Martin continued the theme of girls being strange and mysterious in terms of going to the toilet together, something that Onni suggested that boys could not do without it seeming that 'something actually bad or different is happening'. This then gave the boys the opportunity to do what they like to do and start laughing together. When Marja asked for other examples, Eino identified horse riding as differentiating.

One of the striking features of the co-constructed narrative of difference above is that the boys maintained that they do not know what girls do, or why they do it, but yet seemed to know in detail how they behave in the girls' toilets, the one place in the school where the boys could not see girls. The point is that, across interviews, the boys gave a consistent story of apparently insuperable differences between boys and girls, informal segregation between them and girls being responsible for the segregation despite the fact that boys denigrate girls' activities and friendship groups.

It is not surprising that the boys in the group above said that they had no friends who are girls and that this was because girls are in their own gender-segregated groups. Lauri said, 'I do have the kind of friends as well who are at times with girls. I do go there with them and I don't complain, but I [am] with boys in my free time [laughing].' His suggestion that 'I don't complain' about some of his friends being 'at times' with girls is self-ironic, but suggests that this is something that he tolerated, not that he chose. When Marja asked if the 'activity would be different if there are some girls there?' the boys reiterated the different cultures narrative:

> Lauri: Maybe you can't necessarily make all those sick jokes, [laughs] but you don't usually either if you don't know the people (…)
>
> Onni: Even though there are girls there I don't usually start to change myself because of who is there, but then of course the topics that we talk about, for example at times we talk about video games or something like that. And something that girls might not necessarily understand anything about, so it's not worth talking about those things. I don't change my own behaviour because there are girls there. (*Focus group 5, 5 boys, 14–15 years, four with Finnish background, one with migrant parents, Kukkula School*).

Lauri and Onni pointed out that they behaved in a more controlled way in girls' presence, but that this was not necessarily because of girls' gender but because they did not know girls in the same way as they knew their (male) friends. However, Onni reinforced the notion that the difference also derived from boys' and girls' different interests and that girls 'might not necessarily understand anything about' things that interest boys.

The young people in the sample were at an age where it might be expected that they begin to take an interest in romantic relationships and, for those boys who feel themselves to be heterosexual, that they begin to be interested in spending time with girls despite the strength of many of their narratives of girls' strangeness. Even the boys above who gave strong separatist narratives seemed to indicate that they had spent some time with girls and changed what they talk about, even if not their behaviour in girls' presence. In his individual interview, Yonas – who was one of the few interviewees who actually divulged that he had had a romantic relationship with a girl – made the same point about modulating language and avoiding jokes when spending time with his former girlfriend.

> MP: So is it different to be with a girl than in the friend group, do you chat about different things somehow?
>
> Yonas: Yes and then when you are [with a girl], you behave, you must behave like a bit more calmly and so on. And then, to be a bit more quiet than when you are with your friends, when you're cracking all sorts of jokes and everything like that. And then you have to be, just, a little bit more sensitive. And then we are more quiet and so on. (*Individual interview Yonas, 14 years, Eritrean background, Kukkula School*)

Some boys' narratives gave insights into how the shift to spending time with girls begins to happen and can divide boys in terms of their experiences and desires. In his interview, Bikram, who is two years younger than the boys in the focus group above, made this clear both for mixed-gender friendships and romantic relationships.

> MP: Well you said you have friends who are always hanging out with girls so are there, why do some people have girls as friends and some do not, like is it that they have been friends for a long time or…?
>
> Bikram: I don't know. They just want to talk to them then they have quickly made friends. I have seen something like that since the first day they asked some girls [to join them]. Then I am just like 'why are we asking? This is so

new, and you never do such things'. He said 'who cares let's just try something'. Well now it has been two months and now they are hanging out properly.

MP: Well what do you think would it be nice if you had girls as friends?

Bikram: I have had alright but it's normal. It does not feel weird. It's just the same… It's like a boy. Like I plainly prefer being with boys and so on. (…)

MP: In your class is there something like people who would be dating or that someone would have a girl- or a boy-friend?

Bikram: Yeah one [pair] in our class does. And they get bullied quite a lot. I have noticed that.

MP: For dating?

Bikram: Yeah and like the way that 'you are such a cute couple' and then everyone laughs.

MP: Is the boy your friend?

Bikram: Not a friend but just a guy from our class, I never spend time with him.

MP: What do you think is he–?

Bikram: He is kinda funny but yes a normal guy and so on. (…) I have noticed that if a boy likes a girl he gets bullied, but then if a girl liked a boy then she gets praised for that even more. Like 'go talk to him' and so on, but then boys get bullied for it.

MP: So that boys bully other boys if they, if someone likes?

Bikram: Yea if some boy liked a girl. But if a girl liked a boy, then her friends, like girls they praise her more, I have noticed this.

MP: So that it's a bit embarrassing for a boy to like a girl?

Bikram: I don't know but for example if my friend, like my best friend liked some girl I wouldn't bully him for it, I would tell him like it's good and so on. But others would bully

> about it. (*Individual interview Bikram, 12 years, Nepalese background, Harju School*)

Bikram indicated that he was bemused that other boys want to spend time with girls and that he preferred to spend time only with boys. He also said that a boy who 'likes a girl' and starts to forge relationships with them tends to get bullied by other boys. In giving this account, Bikram pointed out gender differences that he had noticed – that girls are supported by their friends if they like a boy, while boys are censured for wanting romantic relationships with girls. This parallels the inequality discourse discussed earlier, where boys considered girls' allegedly greater freedom of action and interests to be unfair.

## In Conclusion

A major debate in the literature on boys and masculinities is about whether or not the theoretical notion of hegemonic masculinity applies to boys' everyday practices. There is general agreement that there are many versions of masculinities, but disagreement about whether the toughness and homophobia generally reported to characterise boys' everyday practices remains relevant, or whether there is now a more inclusive version of gentler and more homosocial masculinity. Given the strong, long-established norms of gender equality in Finland, it might be expected that inclusive masculinity would be much in evidence in Helsinki schools. In the three schools from which our participants came, however, this was not the case. This chapter has begun to address the issue of hegemonic or inclusive masculinities by considering the participants' perspectives on gender and their views of boys and girls.

The participants in this study showed that they are very familiar with normative understandings of gender equality in Finland. Many produced narratives that espoused what can be viewed as a 'different, but equal' gender ideology. Yet, those same boys also talked of gender in the focus groups and individual interviews in performative ways that constructed girls as inferior to boys and blamed them for the gender segregation that all the participants reported. While the boys took essentialised gender differences for granted, some also considered that boys were unfairly treated. They considered that girls generally had greater freedom to engage in stereotypically girls' activities, and that girls more often than boys were supportive of their friends doing such activities or being romantically interested in boys. It appears, then, that constructing (hegemonic) masculinities in hierarchical relation to girls and femininities remains prevalent in Helsinki schools despite the norms of gender equality. In relation to the issues addressed in the chapter, there is little evidence of inclusive masculinity.

As Roberts and Elliott (2020) pointed out, boys (and men) embodying marginal social positions, such as working-class boys and boys from minoritised ethnic groups, are too often simplistically assumed to be patriarchal, violent and 'toxic'. That this is an oversimplistic view is demonstrated by the fact that many studies find that working-class boys and those from particular racialised/ethnicised groups are frequently considered to embody elements of hegemonic masculinities that many boys find attractive, even if they are not popular (Frosh et al., 2002). Bryan (2020) suggested that US black boys are constrained to behave in ways considered by teachers and white peers to fit within black hegemonic norms, while white boys and girls engage in hegemonic practices that are racialised as well as gendered. In keeping with this, Roberts and Elliott (2020) argued that privileged, white and middle-class boys are implicitly considered normative and so rendered invisible or assumed to be in the vanguard of progressive change, even within critical studies of men and masculinities. In our study, it is important to note that both equality discourses and essentialist discourses that consolidated the hierarchical difference between boys and girls were present in all three schools, despite the different socio-economic and ethnic/'racial' demographics. We thus add to the large literature showing that such juxtapositions oversimplify and essentialise understandings of gender; hierarchising understandings of gender and masculinities are shared across social class and racialised boundaries, as are attempts to nuance them in more equality-oriented discourses (ibid.).

The chapters that follow address other issues that can help illuminate this debate by looking more closely at the differences between boys alongside constructions of gender differences. It is, however, important to recognise that boys' well-worn discourses of gender equality and their treatment of this as axiological might indicate the process of change through potential tensions between their contradictory narratives. This did not appear to be the case since they did not appear to experience the contradictions as problematic. However, it is important to consider the possibility.

CHAPTER 4

# Violence, Popularity and Constructions of Plural Masculinities

In the previous chapter we discussed how the participants constructed differences between boys and girls. However, as has been powerfully shown by many masculinities scholars, boys and men – like people of other genders – are not a uniform group. Instead, they take up different versions of masculinity that are organised hierarchically in relation to each other, and to girls and women. These versions intersect with other aspects of boys' positioning, such as racialisation, ethnicity, social class and other social categories. In this chapter we discuss this hierarchical organisation and differences between boys that were produced in interview discussions on popularity.

The question of which boys are popular is related to the notion of hegemonic masculinities since popular boys are positioned high in power hierarchies of masculinities. Yet, the boys' narratives told a more nuanced story in that they explained that popular boys were not exceptional, as might be expected within theories of 'hegemonic masculinities', but were 'normal' boys who 'do masculinity' through joking and 'stupid things', features that are central to masculine performativity. The question of how popularity is linked to hegemonic masculinities in boys' account is thus more complex than first appears. We focus on it in this chapter because boys in this study, as in a previous study of masculinities in London, treated popularity in similar ways to how hegemonic masculinities are theorised. However, the notion of popularity contains within it both likeability and prestige. Heyder and Kessels (2017) found that boys balance respect earned through fear of violence with likeability. They therefore negotiate how to balance being well known and having prestige (which, Heyder and Kessels found, often comes through fear) and being popular because they are liked. Such findings alert us to the fact that popularity is a complex and contradictory issue that, far from naturally occurring, needs to be worked at. In this chapter, we further unpack some of the elements of hegemony that are much debated in the literature. We start by looking at the role of violence in boys' relationships, and go on to look at narratives where popularity is not based on violence, or fear of it, but likeability in terms of being 'funny'.

## Balancing Violence and Popularity

A central way in which boys and girls are constructed as essentially different is through violence. Maintenance of the hierarchies associated with masculinities and particularly hegemonic masculinities are linked with violence and the threat of violence (Hearn, 2004). These continue to be key cultural markers of masculinity, even among young men in cultures such as Denmark – which, like Finland, consider themselves gender progressive – and despite debates about shifts in the normative boundaries for performing appropriate masculinities (Ravn, 2018). Glimpses from the data on this issue have already been provided in extracts featuring boys who 'always fight in the school corridors' and girls who are considered 'weird' if violent.

Violence and its gendered nature are hard to reconcile with the self-image of Finland as a gender-equal country. This is visible for instance in the frequent media discussions on violence. As this book was being written, in autumn 2020, public debates on violence perpetrated by young people were once again being staged in Finland. One set of discussions were prompted by two serious cases of school violence (e.g. YLE 23.9.2020), another targeted groups or 'gangs' of young people who robbed (mostly) other young people, by using violence or threats of it (e.g. HS 10.11.2020), and yet another related to the homicide of a 16-year-old boy by his three peers, following long-term bullying (HS 18.12.2020). What is noteworthy, but typical, in public discussions on violence in Finland is that, while it may be mentioned that a majority of the young perpetrators are boys or young men, the interlinkage of masculinity and violence is not analysed (Kantola et al., 2011). Regarding the youth violence cases in autumn 2020, public discussion of the causes touched on a variety of topics including the resources available to schools, child protection and increased ethnic diversity, but not on the gender of either perpetrators or victims of violence. Similarly, Kantola, Norocel and Repo (2011) analysed the media discussion of two extreme cases of violence in Finland – the school shootings of 2007 and 2008 – and noted that, while the perpetrators' age, mental health and sociability (or lack of it) were analysed, their (male) gender was left silent, despite its relevance.

While media discussion has not analysed the links between masculinities and violence, there are a few Finnish studies on boys and masculinities, which find a propensity for violence among boys in middle childhood. Manninen, Huuki and Sunnari (2011) found that boys use 'fear power' as a strategic resource and idealise a dominating, hierarchical masculinity. Middle childhood seems to be a pivotal point: Huuki and Sunnari (2015) found that in middle childhood boys are compassionate, but that they become more hierarchical in late childhood, reserving compassion for their 'inner circle' of friends. This relates to similar findings from the USA by Niobe Way (2019), who suggested that it is not that boys stop wanting to have compassionate friendships but that it becomes costly for them in that they come to believe that they cannot trust other boys.

Sari Manninen (2013) found that Finnish boys used violence as a 'respect resource', even though violence was difficult for all boys, those who are marginal and those who are dominant. Manninen introduced the notion of 'banal balancers', which is one of the four 'types' she identified in boys' masculine positionings in relation to violence. 'Banal balancers' behave in ways that enable them to balance being respected through threats of violence and being liked by their peers, both of which are dimensions of status. According to Manninen, they balance between 'too hard' masculinity, which includes, for instance, overt violence, and 'too soft' masculinity in seeking to position themselves as 'ordinary' boys. This balancing requires that boys use violent actions in response to threats and violence targeted at them, which is also linked to their negotiations of popularity. Violence, then, is used to control others and strengthen boys' positioning and is seen as a commonly accepted way of being a boy. This is in keeping with Heyder and Kessels's (2017) finding that boys balance likeability with respect earned through fear of violence (popularity vs prestige).

In this study, as in others, narratives of violence were common and generally discussed as 'playfighting'. This included a variety of masculine performances that were sometimes just for entertainment, like practising wrestling movements or punching each other on the arm. This form of violence is such a normalised part of boys' sociability that it is often not even recognised as violence.

> Samu: [Violence] has never occurred at least in my class, or at least I have never noticed. Of course every now and then there is, like, the kind of pushing around and like this, but it's a bit like play-fighting, like, it doesn't really matter much. (*Individual interview Samu, 13 years, Finnish background, Nurmi School*)

This study diverges from many earlier findings on boys and masculinities in that violence and threat of it were not explicitly discussed as tools for gaining prestige or popularity. However, the normalising of performances of aggression or violence means that such behaviours are also part of what is considered 'normal', 'funny' or 'stupid' by boys. It was, therefore, part of sociability that constructs some boys as popular.

At other times, narratives of violence included an element of conflict. In the following example, Mikael outlined how relatively serious fights are conducted in school.

MP: How it is solved then, if there's a conflict or a fight?

Mikael: I don't know. Usually it works by just saying one time, like, if one is irritated then he usually says, like 'don't do that anymore for real'. And sometimes if there's some kind of fight, someone has touched something then, it may become quite a big [thing], people say.

MP: What sort of things are they then that people get irritated with, or what causes that?

Mikael: Insults, for example if someone has said to a friend something about your parents then it usually really, that may really put you in a trouble because, no one of us for example, we are not interested, because sometimes there might be… Usually it goes like that, that one talks to the other and then we go somewhere outside, in a circle, so that he can't get out of there. Or, like, if someone for real, attacks, then we are able to quickly get them apart.

MP: Is it, do you think it is common for boys that, like violence is used too if someone irritates or like that? Is there a lot something like pushing?

Mikael: Usually we are, like, well my mum has always said that among boys it goes more often like that, one punch and then, for each, and then it is ok, let's settle this. (…) One punch and it's over already, usually. (*Individual interview Mikael, 12 years, mixed parentage, Harju School*)

It is striking that Mikael described a stylised pattern that serves to prevent serious injury or escalation of fights but ensures that fights can happen if there has been a grievance, for example through insult. This lends support to Manninen's (2013) notion of boys' 'banal balancing' of violence as a 'respect resource'. The notion of the circle that other boys form both preventing escape and avoiding serious injury, because other boys can step in to pull opponents apart where necessary, suggests that this is a very well established everyday cultural practice. Equally, in the other kind of fight Mikael explained that his mum had described, the stylised pattern seems to be 'one punch (…) each', limiting the violence to manageable and non-damaging levels, something that Mikael seems to suggest was recognised and sanctioned by his mother. It is also noteworthy that Mikael said that fights may happen 'if someone has said to a friend something about your parents'. A long-standing, common and repeated finding in studies of boys and masculinities is that insults against mothers are an incitement to fight (Frosh et al., 2002; Labov, 1969).

As Ravn (2018) concluded, the boys referred to by Mikael (above) are negotiating the boundary between legitimate and illegitimate physical aggression and how acceptable masculine identities are performed as part of these negotiations in situated ways. These performances allow, and even prescribe, agonistic encounters in certain contexts, in ways that minimise physical harm and are culturally familiar within each school.

## Popular Boys Are Really 'Normal' and Funny

The distinction between popularity and prestige made by some theorists (Heyder and Kessels, 2017) separates being liked and being respected through threat of violence. This is potentially important for advancing understanding of whether individuals who are liked or who are feared are more likely to be hegemonic at school. It is, however, not as easy to disambiguate this as might be expected. Some studies, for example, have found that the most popular boys are those who prioritise popularity and engage in bullying, perhaps because popularity is more precarious for boys than for girls (Duffy et al., 2017). On the other hand, McCormack (2011), in support of inclusive masculinity theory, found that, for 16- to 18-year-old young men in one UK school, popularity was not associated with bullying but with charisma, authenticity, emotional support and social fluidity. These elements are much more about attractiveness and liking than bullying. These contradictory sets of findings may not, however, be incommensurable in that both kinds of characteristics may make boys popular and hegemonically influential, or different institutions may produce different patterns. It may also be that particular versions of popularity are considered hegemonic by boys in different places.

The boys in the Helsinki study provide insights into the complex and multifaceted nature of popularity. In the two examples below, from a focus group and an individual interview, the boys provide a common picture of what constitutes popularity among boys and how it might relate to what researchers consider hegemonic or more inclusive masculinities.

MP: What things make someone popular in school? (…)

Valtteri: It depends a bit on for example if your jokes are really funny and, it can be a bit about what you wear as well and if you're really cool and you have a proper reputation (…) usually actually the popular people in schools are a bit like the kind of really normal people, who are not different at all (…) They hang out in the kind of groups where they are a bit like the leader and then, it is like a badly-behaved boy who's a bit stupid and everything and then everyone laughs.

Kristian: Everyone knows him and it's he-he-he how are you ha-ha.

Valtteri: Of course you can be really popular if everyone just laughs at your bad jokes, and you have to be quite good-looking too. (*Focus group 4, 2 boys, 12 years, Finnish background, Nurmi School*)

MP: Are there those that some people are more popular than others or something that everyone knows them or so?

Yonas: Well yes, it might be.

MP: What do you think what kind of things makes that, that someone becomes popular?

Yonas: Well he's doing something funny or something like that. And when everyone laughs, then everyone knows someone. Yeah.

MP: Some jokes or…?

Yonas: Yes or doing some stupid things sometimes too. (*Individual interview Yonas, 14 years, Eritrean background, Kukkula School*)

Across the two extracts, from boys aged 12 and 14 years, the elements they pick out indicate that popular boys are likeable, famous and prestigious, but violence and threat are never mentioned as conferring popularity. Instead, the boys pick out elements that boys suggest are central to masculinity: telling (bad) jokes that make lots of other boys laugh so that they become well known in the school for this, but also having a reputation for doing 'stupid things'. Doing 'stupid things' seems to be much admired by boys in the same way that being funny also is. It seems to be about doing slightly risky things that resist authority in minor ways, and so being 'badly behaved' without incurring serious punishments. In addition, popular boys are said to be 'cool', wear things that make them popular and are quite good looking.

Valtteri's account in his focus group is particularly notable because he highlights an issue that is debated in the literature on hegemonic masculinities: their (un)attainability for ordinary men and boys. Valtteri suggests that popular boys are 'like the kind of really normal people, who are not different at all'. In other words, they are not so different from most other boys. They are not superstars or super tough, even though they 'hang out in the kind of groups where they are a bit like the leader'.

The socio-economic differences between the areas where the schools were located were present in details of narratives of popularity and style or appearances. The intersections of popularity and socio-economic status were salient in Nurmi School, located in a very affluent area, as Samu made clear:

MP: What do you think that here in school so what makes, like someone already like popular? If you think about boys so what kind of boys are usually popular?

Samu: Well I don't know probably like the ones who like, usually it is, that when you are rich, so from that you get that then you can afford to do everything cool in a way, even though you can do everything cool without the money as well, but usually it's quite a big thing, that I do know from this school as well people who are so rich that they are popular because of that. But then it's of course there

> are some exceptions to it like there are rich [people] but they are not that popular. And then usually in relation to the money so then there are specific clothes that you get. (*Individual interview Samu, 13 years, Finnish background, Nurmi School*)

From Samu's account, it is easier for boys to be popular if they are 'rich' and can both afford 'specific clothes' and 'do everything in a cool way'. So, while he was careful to make clear that boys who are rich are not necessarily popular and that boys can 'do everything cool without money', he highlighted the intersection of money and popularity. This is another instance of popularity not being related to toughness or violence. The affluence of the area of Nurmi School also meant that participants whose families were not as wealthy as some other families on the area might feel that they did not have quite the same opportunities for consumption than their peers:

> Daniel: Well... I can't call us [his family] rich but we cannot be compared to the poor either.
>
> MP: Right. Do you think it matters that, if you have a lot of money or not?
>
> Daniel: It is like, like when I live on quite a rich area, so quite many people here buy different things that I really can't... like, we can't really afford.
>
> MP: Okay, you mean there are lots of guys in this area who are much richer?
>
> Daniel: Yes.
>
> MP: Okay. What kind of things they are then?
>
> Daniel: Well like, one of my... I know one boy who bought a while ago shoes that cost a thousand euros.
>
> MP: Huh. Well quite few people can afford that.
>
> Daniel: Yes but... here you see quite many of them. (*Individual interview, Daniel, 12 years, mixed parentage, Nurmi School*)

While certain brand products were valued, *bragging* with money or expensive products was considered tasteless and not 'cool'. Thus, exclusive brands worked as a tool in gaining popularity only if combined with nonchalance that also marked 'authentic' masculinity. Investing in style was risky also because, if seen as excessive, it was sometimes regarded as 'gay'. As Daniel again explained, 'for example one guy (…) he bought a shirt with long sleeves that cost 160 euros and is black and white striped so we were all like, everybody said a bit like, irritating, it is a way to irritate that guy to say that he is, like, a gay' (see more on name-calling in Chapter 5).

Style and brands were not insignificant in the two other schools either; however, the brands that were referred to were quite different ones and less exclusive than the brands discussed in Nurmi School. Further, unlike in Nurmi School, in both Kukkula and Harju Schools the participants spoke about how wearing 'fake' brand clothes or shoes was disdained at school and a potential reason for bullying. As Harvey and colleagues (2013) argued in their analysis on 'swagger' or knowledge and style that work as capital in masculine hierarchies, social class is constructed through style and, in order to be valued, 'swagger' needs to be proved authentic. 'Fake' brand clothes do not work as capital in masculine hierarchies since they do not signify wealth but rather lack of it (ibid.) and they are also connected with inauthenticity. The question of style and appearances thus bring out the importance of social class in masculine popularity. The relationships between popularity and style and appearances are complex; in order to be valued, the investment in style always needs to be balanced with performances of masculine 'authenticity' in order to not be seen as excessive, girly or gay. While none of the boys cited above linked popularity with racialisation, it becomes clear in the discussion of multiculturalism that a further intersection with popularity is to do with racialisation in that black boys are not viewed as popular (see Chapter 8).

It is notable that popularity was not generally talked about as embodied in actual boys present in the focus groups or other named boys, which would open up the possibility for focus group participants to compare whether they consider the same boys popular. Rather exceptionally, however, Daniel, Jaakko and Elmeri negotiate which of them is 'the most popular', focusing on Daniel and Elmeri, who are present:

> MP: Okay. How do you feel yourself, like, are you so-called popular or, semi?
>
> Daniel: Well like I am. [a bit quiet; this gets mixed up with others talking]
>
> Jaakko: Elmeri is—
>
> Elmeri: Well like, probably Daniel is the most popular of us really.
>
> Daniel: No.
>
> Elmeri: How come, well who then?
>
> Daniel: You.
>
> Elmeri: How come?
>
> Jaakko: Aren't you the Brad Pitt of our class?
>
> Aleksi: Yeah.
>
> Elmeri: [laughs] (*Focus group 3, 4 boys, 13 years, three with Finnish background, one mixed parentage, Nurmi School*)

The above extract shows the ambivalence involved in negotiating the position of 'the most popular one'. No one wanted to be seen to claim that position, even if they may have wanted to be 'popular' (e.g. Daniel). It is noteworthy that Jaakko's question to Elmeri, 'Aren't you the Brad Pitt of our class?', contained within it the seeds of a compliment but was not necessarily designed to be complimentary. It verged on ridiculing Elmeri in a passive-aggressive way without eliciting aggression from Elmeri because of the ubiquity of boys' joking practices and because it was couched in ways that could be defended as complimentary if Elmeri had expressed anger. Not surprisingly, Elmeri's somewhat awkward laugh brought an end to this discussion since it put Elmeri in a troubled subject position (Wetherell, 1998) where he could not agree without seeming vain and opening himself to ridicule, and he could not demur without also possibly being teased or diminishing his status. It may be that Aleksi saved him from embarrassment by simply saying 'Yeah'.

In another case, a group of sixth-grade boys in Harju School described the whole group of sixth-graders – thus including themselves – as being at the top of the school hierarchy. In further discussion, they pointed out that popularity was also related to being sporty; however, since they all self-identified as both sixth-graders and sporty, this did not create (or identify) hierarchies within the focus group itself.

> Bikram: Everyone knows the sixth graders and so on. (…)
>
> MP: You are the bosses?
>
> Bikram: In a way.
>
> Mikael: Basically.
>
> MP: So among the sixth graders, is there something…?
>
> Mikael: Depends, on what you are interested in and what you do and for example quite a few of us, like to play football or so.
>
> Bikram: Yea in our school.
>
> Luka: Some scoot.
>
> Bikram: Yea riding a scooter and so on.
>
> Elias: Or sports.
>
> Mikael: Yea sports but if you do not like it then.
>
> Bikram: Yea if you think about it we boys at the sixth grade are quite sporty and so on, quite a lot. For example almost every boy is, has some kinda hobby.
>
> Elias: Yea and does a lot of sports. (*Focus group 6, 5 boys, 12 years, one with Finnish background, two with migrant parents, two mixed parentage, Harju School*)

Thus, even when some boys were named as 'popular', it was rare for them to make visible a hierarchy that could indicate hegemonic masculinity. In the rare case when boys named themselves or others as popular, they appeared to have marked difficulties in establishing a hierarchy and claiming hegemony. This may be related to the fact that popularity is a vague and shifting category in parallel ways to the slipperiness of hegemonic masculinity. It is also a risky category for boys. As found in other studies, being the most popular person is a precarious position, inviting contestation or even ridicule (Duffy et al., 2017).

What, then, of the question of whether masculinities are becoming more inclusive? The boys' accounts also throw light on this issue. In the extract below, from a focus group, Onni and Eino nuanced the notion of popularity by distinguishing between liking and infamy.

> Onni: If we talk about being popular for real in that way that they're liked more, so usually it's not like a troublemaker because that is exactly the kind of person who you don't necessarily like that much.
>
> Eino: For example, I wouldn't probably otherwise know a couple of people from A and B class if they hadn't disturbed the lesson, so I've heard about them that they have again done this and again done that, and so on. But anyway I don't know if they are popular, but I've just heard about them.
>
> Onni: I think popular and well-known are a different thing. (*Focus group 5, 5 boys, 14–15 years, four with Finnish background, one with migrant parents, Kukkula School*)

Onni made an explicit distinction between popularity and being well known, particularly if people are well known for being troublemakers. Eino identified people from two other classrooms who were infamous only because they disturb lessons and are disruptive in other ways. He explained that he did not know if these boys were popular, implying that they were not popular with him. From all the examples, it does not seem that toughness or violence was part of hegemony for the boys in the study and there appear to be limits to the disruptiveness that boys consider endearing.

One aspect of the theorisation of hegemonic masculinity is that it sets the normative standard of masculinity that other boys and men desire. This is, however, not necessarily the case since some boys made it clear that they did not aspire to be among the most popular in school.

> Veeti: Yeah. But I don't maybe think of it as the world's best [thing to be the] most popular, so rather you want to be the not-so-popular if you just keep yourself as like a sensible person. So if you tried some stupid things… yeah. (*Individual interview Veeti 13 years, Finnish background, Nurmi School*)

> MP: Well is it for you like that if you think, like for you yourselves, is it like something which would be a good thing?
>
> Valtteri: Well no, I wouldn't want to be popular at all.
>
> MP: Okay, why not?
>
> Valtteri: Somehow like, I'm not interested in that kind of life, like I'd rather be—
>
> Kristian: Just a tough guy.
>
> Valtteri: No but, just myself, and not any, [not to] pretend to be the kind of *jonne* [lad] who does everything to be popular. (*Focus group 4, 2 boys, 12 years, Finnish background, Nurmi School*)

In the extracts above, the boys explained that they did not want to be popular. Veeti's philosophy was that he would rather be the 'not-so-popular' one so that he could 'keep [himself] as like a sensible person'. It is not that he wanted to be unpopular but that he saw the costs of being visibly popular as too great. In this, his account fits with findings from various studies that hegemonic masculinities have costs for boys and men who have to live up to particular ways of behaving that prove costly to themselves (Fergus and Bennett, 2018; Majors and Billson, 1993; Way, 2019). For Valtteri, popular masculinity was inauthentic and requires commitment to working for popularity, something that Duffy et al. (2017) also suggested. Instead, he said that he would prefer to be just himself. For the boys in the study, then, popularity was not necessarily desirable for themselves. These accounts run counter to McCormack's (2011) findings that popular boys are supportive of other boys and do not court popularity. The boys in this study indicated that popularity had to be worked at and, while they liked the jocular aspects of popular masculinity, they did not want the constraints that would accrue from having to keep working at being popular.

The sections above show that boys are very familiar with the signifiers of masculinities and popular masculinity. Yet, most were reluctant to position themselves as, or aspire to, being popular themselves. They considered its contradictions too difficult to negotiate as they worked to maintain their positioning in masculine hierarchies.

## In Conclusion

Fame, likeability, daring, resistance, toughness, violence and hierarchy are all part of the theorisation of 'hegemonic masculinities'. The younger boys did talk of both playfighting and more serious fighting that was limited in its violence because there appeared to be formulaic patterns that reduced its potential danger. They could, therefore, be considered 'banal balancers' of violence in Manninen's (2013) terms. Older boys did not mention fighting in these ways (although, with a small sample, it is not possible to be definite about whether this is a general age difference). In this study, as in others, we asked what made boys popular. The answers were consistent across year groups, individual and focus group interviews and boys from different ethnicised groups. Popular boys were mostly not individually identified. However, the characteristics the boys associated with popularity were telling (bad) jokes that gained fame, being 'cool' in dress and practices and some resistant or disruptive behaviour that gave them infamy so that boys gained social status and prestige for being rebellious. Mild rebelliousness was the closest boys reported coming to the toughness that is commonly found to be an aspect of hegemonic masculinities in other countries.

Much literature on popularity points to violence and so fear as part of what makes boys popular and keeps them high in masculine hierarchies. This was never identified by boys in the Helsinki study. Bullying and fear were not mentioned in association with popularity. Perhaps surprisingly, given that hegemonic masculinities are said to organise boys' and men's positioning and desires, boys did not necessarily aspire to be very popular on the grounds that they wanted to be somewhat 'sensible' or authentically themselves (viewing popularity as necessarily disruptive). This did not mean that their everyday practices were not constrained and facilitated by notions of what boys should be like. As is clear in all the empirical chapters, whatever the issue being discussed, boys were keen to make distinctions between themselves and girls, as well as to ensure that they were included as belonging among the 'normal' boys. In order to negotiate their masculine positions, they had to be able to make and take jokes, funniness being an important part of likeability and masculinities. The boys in the study were not keen to stand apart from other boys in ways that would fit with theorisations of hegemonic masculinity or could be defined by other boys as 'weird'. It was, therefore, difficult for them to claim popularity for themselves.

CHAPTER 5

# Homosocial Relationships: Peers and Friends

As we saw in Chapters 1 and 3, boys' relationships with other boys are central to their positioning in masculinities. The long-standing finding that boys at school commonly call each other 'gay' fits with the theorisation of homophobia as central to hegemonic masculinity. However, findings that, in some schools, boys are able to hug each other and to be gently considerate of boys who do not fit with the characteristics of hegemonic masculinity led Anderson (2009) to argue that there is now an 'inclusive masculinity' that does not rely on homophobia. This claim has been much disputed and there is ample evidence that homophobic name-calling continues to be a mundane feature of boys' social relationships (Odenbring and Johansson, 2021). However, evidence that some boys resist homophobic practices indicates that the social changes that have characterised the 2000s may be inflecting boys' relationships at school in many countries (Bhana and Mayeza, 2019; Francis and Kjaran, 2020). This chapter focuses on the ways in which boys' social relations with their peers were patterned. It aims to understand the complexity of their relations and consistencies and contradictions in the ways in which they 'do' masculinities in relation to their peers and friends.

The term 'homosocial' was popularised by Eve Kosofsky Sedgwick (1985) to refer to male social, non-sexual relationships. This form of male bonding she theorised as often being accompanied by a fear or hatred of homosexuality. Homosociality is thus not necessarily inclusive in the non-homophobic way McCormack and Anderson (2010) suggested. As we shall see, boys were generally committed to maintaining inclusive masculine friendships within their school classes in terms of seeing all boys as friends. It was important to many that 'boys are friends with all boys'. Joking, a key element of 'popular masculinity', was a central mechanism through which friendly social relationships were established and maintained. Their positive norm of sociability did not mean, however, that boys opposed the use of 'gay' as an insult to other boys. Nor did it mean that friendships were intimate or confiding. As Niobe Way (2011) has repeatedly found in her research on US boys, in their adolescence and later on, very few felt that they could confide in their friends. The few who said they could were selective about who they confided in and what they confided. The boys identified this as a difference between boys and girls, since they considered that girls routinely confided in their friends.

Friendly relations are clearly important to boys in affording them pleasurable interactions, fun and a sense of belonging that made school liveable (Butler, 2004). This is not, however, the whole story in that friendly relations (as with all social relations) are multifaceted. The chapter argues that the reason that boys were deeply invested in maintaining friendly relations with all other boys was because failure to do so would potentially open them to teasing interactions and name-calling. They reported that both of these were common among boys. It was an insurance policy against being lonely when they changed schools since, if they were friendly with all boys, they were likely to find themselves in the same class as some boys with whom they were already friends. It also guaranteed protection for most boys from being viewed as unvalued outsiders since, if all boys were friends with all other boys, they were automatically included in friendship groups. It is noteworthy, however, that two boys in the study appeared to have no friends; the norm of sociability thus did not equally protect all boys.

The boys' accounts suggest that, although, as discussed in Chapter 4, the boys claimed that they did not seek popularity, popularity nonetheless serves to organise boys' everyday practices because it is a systematically vague concept, including fame (visibility), prestige, likeability, daring, resistance, toughness and dominance (Heyder and Kessels, 2017). All of these are part of 'hegemonic masculinities', but each can be detached from other elements of popularity. Admiration, liking, hate and fear are all sedimented into popularity, which organises many boys' (self-) positioning and desires in the ways hegemonic masculinities are reported to do (Connell and Messerschmidt, 2005). For the boys in the study, for example, likeability was important to some extent since they needed to be able to claim friendship with all boys.

This chapter is divided into four main sections. It first discusses inclusive homosociality and the ways in which inclusiveness was limited, rather than including all versions of masculinities. It then considers the ways in which joking and name-calling constitute a central way in which boys 'do' masculinities and the hierarchies of hegemonic masculinities are maintained. The third section considers gaming as a form of masculine sociality that many boys considered characterised masculinity, even though they recognised that some girls are gamers. The final main section addresses the issue of whether or not boys had close, confiding relationships and could share their thoughts and emotions with friends. That section provides a bridge to Chapter 7, on family relationships, since both address boys' access to, and desire (or lack of desire) for, close relationships, first with friends and then with parents and siblings.

## Inclusive Homosociality and Its Limits

Many boys' narratives demonstrated a commitment to maintaining friendly relationships with 'all' or most boys in their class. Thirteen-year-old Johannes summed up this sentiment, saying, 'Well like, probably boys have it that, or at least I feel that boys are, a little bit like, friends with every boy. Unless they are really, like, irritating.'

Sociality was widely valued, and most boys described themselves as social and as having many friends. Friendships and friendly relations were important in themselves, but they were also important in that they acted as 'insurance' against being seen as alone and at the bottom of the social hierarchy. Martin's narrative was very insightful in explaining that it is in his interest to be a part of all the social groupings in his class – if only peripherally.

> MP: And if you think about the other boys in the school? Are there people with whom you get along worse or, better? What different kind of boys are there in the school?
>
> Martin: Every boy has their own group that they belong to. And then I belong to, as for me it is a bit, in my interest to belong a bit to all the groups, but not so that every group would like me a lot, but they do like me. (…)
>
> MP: Do some have more friends than others?
>
> Martin: No. Everyone tries to be friends with everybody, because once you are with the same group, you get to know everyone and maybe then you do not get into the same school, you get lonely.
>
> MP: Do you think that there are many lonely people? Students?
>
> Martin: Everyone is lonely on the inside. (*Individual interview Martin, 15 years, Estonian background, Kukkula School*)

Martin's thoughtful, open account lends itself to a psychosocial analysis in that he presents his emotions, as well as his social positioning. It becomes clear early in the above extract that Martin feels himself to be somewhat an outsider in saying that 'Every boy has their own group that they belong to', but making himself an exception and explaining that it is in his interest 'to belong a bit to all the groups'. This sounds defensive, as if he sought to belong to all the groups to protect himself from being a disliked outsider. He did not claim to be liked 'very much' but asserted that he was liked. He also denied that some boys have more friends than others on the grounds that boys get to know everyone in their groups. He suggested that all boys sought to be friends with everybody, because having extensive social networks prevents loneliness. His response that 'Everyone is lonely on the inside' is both poignant and suggests that he was lonely in school.

In support of this, Martin is one of the two boys in the study who considered that they did not have any friends.

Despite Martin's felt outsider status, the boys in the study told a pervasive story that emphasised an inclusive masculine sociality. Inclusivity was explicitly described as a masculine feature of social relationships, and contrasted with girls' (assumed) tendency to spend time in smaller groups and form 'cliques'. The boys' narratives stressed the irrelevance of their friends' backgrounds and opinions and explained that what mattered for friendships was how the friends get along; a friend was someone one was able to have fun with.

> MP: Are your friends usually somehow, are they certain type of boys or are they all different?
>
> Aleksi: Not really, I… don't like to define my friends in a way according to their opinions, or I do a bit like that, but… I'm friends with those I get along well with and I have fun with, so anything else doesn't basically matter. (…)
>
> MP: So about ethnic backgrounds amongst your friends, does it matter at all, that, what is someone's skin colour or where there are from?
>
> Aleksi: Noo. To me the main thing is that you're a cool person and then like, funny jokes [stories] and you get along. So that is in a way to me for example makes no difference if someone for example, likes some ballet and I don't, but as long as I get along with them otherwise. (*Individual interview Aleksi, 12 years, Finnish background, Nurmi School*)

Aleksi made a strong case for opinions, backgrounds and activities not mattering, and in mentioning ballet as a potentially acceptable interest for a friend highlighted inclusivity and his openness towards different and also less traditional masculinities. He did, however, nuance his account. For example, he said that he did define his friends 'a bit like that' (on their opinions). At the same time, he referred to ballet as very far from his own interests and an extreme case that would usually be considered outside masculinity. In so doing, he reaffirmed his own masculinity through distancing himself from ballet and belied his strong claim that 'it makes no difference'. Further, Aleksi implicitly constructed boys who like ballet as different from himself and less normative in terms of masculinity. Since he brought up boys who like ballet in response to Marja's question on the significance of ethnicity or skin colour in friendships, this implicitly suggests that these differences are significant in distancing boys from each other and also signify non-normative masculinity. This is despite the fact that he constructed shared fun as being sufficient to bridge ethnicised differences.

Studies on boys and masculinities have repeatedly discussed the finding that involvement in activities – doing things together – is a marker of masculinity, while interacting through talk – discussing, sharing thoughts and emotions – is considered more feminine (e.g. de Boise and Hearn, 2017; Edwards, 2004; Gordon et al., 2000; Thorne, 1993). Particular school contexts allow and encourage different activities. In one of the schools in this study, Harju, many of the boys used to play football together during the breaks. In Kukkula School, 'all' boys gathered around a ping-pong table to play and to socialise during the breaks. In both contexts girls occasionally came to join the activity. Their presence was tolerated by the boys as strange but acceptable exceptions to what they largely considered masculine activities. Shared activity helped boys to maintain an inclusive masculine sociality, which, according to many boys' accounts, mostly ignored individual differences. This is illustrated by a quote from Liban's interview:

MP: What about here in school, do you see here, like, different groupings of boys?

Liban: Well I think that we are all different, but then when we are here in school everybody, like hangs out, like nobody minds even though you are at the same time, or nobody cares what is your opinion, you know. Because, for instance, if we are all like a bit different, for instance, I have my own opinion, but then when the break begins, we all gather around the ping pong table and we all play, you know, so that it doesn't really matter what you think. (...)

MP: Is it here, is it usually just boys who hang out there around the ping pong table?

Liban: Well not necessarily. Sometimes some girls come, like, 'we want to play', then we are just like, in a fair way, so that everybody queues, so then we are like, 'if you go there at the end of the queue then you can play'. (*Individual interview Liban, 14 years, Somali background, Kukkula School*)

As Liban made clear, girls who wanted to join what the boys viewed as boys' activities were viewed as exceptional, even though they were treated fairly and allowed to take a turn. Among boys, though, a joint activity is able to temporarily render individual differences irrelevant.

Contrary to the boys' canonical narrative that opinions and activities are irrelevant to friendships and that they socialised with 'all' boys, there were hierarchies of masculinities in the schools in that certain boys' friendships and company were reported to be less valued than others'. When asked what made boys vulnerable to being alone, unpopular or bullied, the boys listed a number of things, many of which were connected to boys' bodies and ways of being masculine. These characteristics included: being short, looking young, not being sporty or fit, having a physical defect or a disease, 'girly' hobbies, using 'fake' brand clothes, getting angry easily, or not being able to take a joke. According to some, any difference or acting in a 'weird' or 'irritating' way exposed boys to bullying. Even though only a minority of boys spontaneously mentioned the risk of being labelled as gay, when asked, everybody agreed that questioning accepted masculine norms (through behaviour or interests that could be interpreted as 'girly') would lead to laughter and being called 'gay'. Inasmuch as the reasons for exclusion or bullying concerned clothing and style, they clearly also intersected with social class and different opportunities for consumption, as did the markers of popularity (see e.g. Harvey et al., 2013 and Chapter 4). Even though many of the boys interviewed were critical of this kind of hierarchisation and labelling, they considered it an inevitable and mundane part of school life and did not challenge it.

The supposed irrelevance of difference to masculine sociality was also mentioned by Sami, a transgender boy. However, in his narrative this did not increase the inclusiveness of boy groups but was produced by the boys' conformity to masculine norms that flattened out differences and gave them a uniform appearance:

> Sami: I mean I know some of them, some of them are really nice but then when they move there in the corridors in the boy groups, so you notice that they all have the same kind of clothes, all have the same kind of everything. And then someone cuts their hair in a specific way so someone else gets the same thing the next week and you are just looking from the side that wow, oh well hey. Then I don't even know anyone's names when they're just one. (*Focus group 7, a girl and trans boy, 15 years, Finnish background, Keinu youth club*)

While masculine sociality may render some differences irrelevant (although, as seen above, this can be contradicted by what the boys say), for Sami it was clear that he was not included by boys as properly masculine: 'It is difficult to hang out with the boys sometimes, there is always that kind of, that "you are a girl, you don't know this thing going on"'.

Given the strength of the norm of sociality and being friends and young people's general tendency to understand lack of friends as entailing exclusion (Myllyniemi, 2009), it was not easy for the young people to talk about having no friends and being lonely. Martin (discussed above) and Joel were, therefore, exceptional in the study in explaining that they practically had no friends. Joel, for instance, first says that the boys in his class are his friends ('basically') and so are the people in his extra-curricular music hobby. None of these people is, however, sufficiently close for him to spend time with them outside the school and hobby contexts.

MP: Can you describe yourself a bit, what kind of person you are in general?

Joel: Maybe a quiet one. [very quietly, apologetic laugh] I don't know.

MP: But there is, of course, nothing wrong with that. Do you have friends here in the school?

Joel: Yes. The boys in the class, basically. (…)

MP: Do you have friends outside school?

Joel: Well. Well basically the guys of the [music hobby]. The band.

MP: From the music hobby.

Joel: Yes, but I'm never with them, or actually I'm never with my friends anyway. (*Individual interview Joel, 14 years, Finnish background, Kukkula School*)

For many reasons, Joel had limited possibilities to embody 'hegemonic' masculinity. He identified as a quiet boy, which suggests that he did not find masculine joking – an essential part of masculine sociality (e.g. Huuki et al., 2010; Kehily and Nayak 1997) – easy or 'natural'. Joel's family situation was also not easy either economically or with regard to social relationships, and he considered it more important to spend time with his mother than with his peers.

In summary, sociality and 'getting along' were norms that encouraged boys to 'be friends with everybody'. Friendships and masculine sociality provided company, pleasure and fun, and protected the boys from loneliness and ending up at the bottom of the masculine hierarchy. However, while boys emphasised that (some) differences between boys did not matter, not all boys could claim inclusion and belonging, and the company of some was valued more than others. These differences between boys highlighted their intersectional positioning, as they were related not only to norms and hierarchies of masculinities, but to social class, (cis/trans) gender, and 'race' and ethnicity.

## Joking and Name-Calling

Besides shared physical activities, a central part of masculine sociality and boys' friendships was joking (see also Barnes, 2012; Huuki et al., 2010; Kehily and Nayak, 1997). Joking was a way to spend time in itself and an integral part of many activities. It was what made hanging out with other boy(s) fun. Joking had many positive functions: shared joking was a form that included others. It was a sign of being close to someone and a way to share observations and (positive) emotions. However, joking was also a way to mark difference, to ridicule others and to establish (masculine) hierarchy.

Joking works only when those present 'get' the joke. The masculine norms in all three schools required that boys should not be offended by jokes, even when they were racist, homophobic or otherwise offensive. Many participants recognised the contradictory functions of joking, and they knew that people interpreted 'jokes' in different ways and that some 'jokes' were meant to be insults. Humour is thus an important but ambivalent part of boys' everyday life – it can be used for inclusive community-building, for othering and de-valuing others, and for shaking and questioning hierarchies (Huuki et al., 2010). An extract from a focus group interview with five boys illustrates the contradictory nature of joking as a part of masculine sociality. Bikram first talks about bullying in a disapproving way, even though he suggests that those bullied and bullying in other groups did not care about it. However, when the narrative turns to social practices in the participants' own group, practices looking very similar to those examples of bullying were described as 'only joking'. The boys were self-critical in recognising that, for those who are not familiar with a group, this may be experienced as insulting and saddening:

Bikram: I have noticed that in some groups of friends, the strategy is that, for example, someone is being bullied, well even the bullied one does not care 'cause he is in a group in which they bully each other. So he doesn't care, and he starts bullying them too.

Elias: Yea like kind of joking around.

Bikram: Yea like joking around. But then in some, like our group is like this, that we for example call each other names but no one cares. But then some new guys we do not really know what they are like so, they could for example get sad real fast and get offended.

Luka: Yea.

Mikael: Yea.

Bikram: So then in a way we do not know that.

Mikael: And then as we do not get that we just [keep] joking around.

Bikram: Yea we do not get it.

Mikael: Yea.

Bikram: But for example between us we can call each other names, because nobody cares.

Mikael: And it is not even really calling names—

Bikram: No since—

Luka: It is just kind of joking around.

Bikram: Yea joking around. Like we get the joke and so on, but not everyone necessarily does. (*Focus group 6, 5 boys, 12 years, one with Finnish background, two with migrant parents, two mixed parentage, Harju School*)

What is also important in the quote is the way that joking marks the borders of friendships: joking is considered possible in a stronger way within friendship groups. Between friends, everybody is expected to 'get' the joke. It was repeatedly stated that one had to be more on guard with less close acquaintances – and with girls who did not know when what was being said was a joke.

The boys' narratives show that joking is a masculine practice that defines who is included as a 'friend' or an 'outsider', and creates a strong masculine norm of being able to 'take a joke' and not complaining over 'minor' things. Even when joking bordered or overlapped with bullying, it was often considered an inevitable part of sociality that boys had to, and did, get used to, or at least put up with:

> MP: Well you said, that every now and then people playfully wind each other up for some reason?
>
> Yonas: For example when, you have done something, something like a bit embarrassing or basically, so after a while maybe a week or something, then people start to, like, make fun of that or they play the fool about that thing with you.
>
> MP: So someone remembers that and then he says something about it?
>
> Yonas: And then everyone is laughing and so.
>
> MP: Right. Has that ever happened to you?
>
> Yonas: Yes it has. Yeah.
>
> MP: How did it feel, is it a bit embarrassing or?
>
> Yonas: Well, like. We are kind of used to that so it is not so embarrassing any more like it was, at the beginning. (*Individual interview Yonas, 14 years, Eritrean background, Kukkula School*)

Even though joking clearly was very important, calling something 'only joking' was also a way to use claims that it is not serious or worth complaining about to discipline boys into normative versions of masculinities and maintain the centrality of hegemonic masculinities. This line of argument blurred the line between bullying and joking and made the social control exercised through joking harder to resist. Discussions of calling someone 'gay' provide an illustrative case of how calling something 'a joke' enables disciplining and policing of 'proper masculinity' through homophobic practices that otherwise would be considered unacceptable. Homophobic name-calling has a long history and has been found to be a central, widespread practice for policing heterosexual masculinity among young people in numerous research projects (e.g. Frosh, Phoenix and Pattman, 2002; Kehily and Nayak, 1997;

Lehtonen, 2002; Pascoe, 2005). While some researchers have identified the emergence of new, more inclusive and less homophobic masculinities (Anderson 2009), in the light of these data it seems too soon and too optimistic to valorise such ideas as marking a turning point for young masculinities. In this study, all the interviewees acknowledged that the term 'gay' was a widely used insult in their daily lives.

> MP: In other schools ... we have talked about this thing of calling someone gay, that boys still use it as a word of abuse?
>
> Lauri: It's probably the most common word of abuse [laughter].
>
> Onni: It's usually added like after a word or like–
>
> Lauri: Hey gay [laughing]
>
> Onni: Yeah like that added after a word, like for example are you some figure-skating gay or something like that, so it's added there after so not as an individual word, but like, it's always added after some thing that you do. (...)
>
> Lauri: Or then it might be that if you have for example new shoes or a new shirt or something like that, so they might say that the new shoes look gay or like that. [laughing] (*Focus group 5, 5 boys, 14–15 years, four with Finnish background, one with migrant parents, Kukkula School*)

Even though several boys claimed that 'gay' is used as a generic insult that does not 'really mean anything', the examples provided by Onni and Lauri illustrate well how the term is used for controlling what can be seen as appropriate forms of masculinity and for disciplining those boys whose interests or appearance do not match with the ideals of heterosexual/hegemonic masculinity. At the level of everyday practices, homophobia remains integral to ideas of 'proper' masculinity among teenage boys (see also Pascoe, 2005).

This was, however, not the whole story. Discussions on homophobic name-calling exposed important contradictions. While the interviewees reported hearing it and sometimes using it themselves, almost all were critical of it. Calling someone 'gay' as an insult was repeatedly described as 'stupid', 'weird', 'only a joke' and 'not effective as an insult'. For instance, for Valtteri calling someone 'gay' as an insult was old-fashioned and did not correspond to the real meaning of the word:

> Valtteri: Even in this class they call each other gay quite a lot like that, but it's a bit like more as a joke like that. They do usually, I've been called gay quite many times in this school, so, yeah.
>
> MP: Well what do you think about [the fact] that gay is like a word of abuse?
>
> Valtteri: It's not really, it was maybe sometime in the 90s a thing but like, those dudes still call people gays [in a negative way], it's a bit like an old thing that, when it's not even, originally [it] hasn't been a word of abuse so, they should figure out a new word of abuse for example. (*Focus group 4, 2 boys, 12 years, Finnish background, Nurmi School*)

Unlike in some earlier studies (e.g. Frosh et al., 2002), it seemed to be relatively easy for the participants to tell the researcher that they had been called 'gay' (albeit only as 'a joke'!). Further, two participants actively brought up their queer identities and, rather than feeling that they had to hide them, they explained that they had tried to create more positive ways of using the term 'gay' as a form of resistance to the homophobic discourses at the school:

> Sami: I have in fact challenged these situations for example at one point one guy from our class said something, 'fucking gay' or something like that, so I was like 'Excuse me, were you talking to me?'. And yes, in that way I came out to my class. [laughs] (…) I have in fact used [the term 'gay'] also in a kind of opposite way, that I have used it positively with people hearing, and about myself in a positive way. That I try a little to take the word onto

myself and get them to understand that in my opinion it's a good word.

Katriina: Yes, and I said to Leena one day that 'you look very gay today' and she said 'thank you'. [laughs] (*Focus group 7, a girl and trans boy, 15 years, Finnish background, Keinu youth club*)

Homophobic name-calling does, then, still act as a way to police boys' ways of being masculine, even though this may be less absolute and less shaming than in previous decades. Our observations are in line with Pascoe's (2005) analysis of how the derogatory term 'fag' continues to work as 'an abject position outside of masculinity that actually constitutes masculinity' (p. 342). According to Pascoe, the term may or may not relate to boys' sexual orientation, but it always carries meanings of not being properly masculine. It thus remains a way of controlling how boys 'do gender' that does not work in a symmetrical way for girls. 'Gay' was used only very exceptionally for girls (see above, however). A closely parallel way of controlling girls' femininities seemed to be using insulting words related to girls' excessive (hetero)sexuality, as has been found in the literature on 'slags', 'sluts' and 'slut-shaming' and gendered social control of girls (e.g. Cawie and Lees, 1981; Ringrose and Renold, 2012):

MP: It's probably the kind of word of abuse that is used precisely for boys I presume?

Martin: Yeah. (…)

Onni: I don't know if girls have some word, slut or something common like that. [laughter] I don't know I haven't heard…

Lauri: You are such sluts. [laughing] [Joint laughter]

Onni: Or like, but that's how girls mock each other with that, not like 'you look like a…' but, mock each other with that word then, I don't know. (*Focus group 5, 5 boys, 14–15 years, four with Finnish background, one with migrant parents, Kukkula School*)

As with using the term 'gay' as an insult, using 'slut' did not constitute an allegation that the person being abused engaged in the sexual practices being referred to. Nevertheless, both terms serve to sanction certain ways of 'doing gender' and illustrate the different ideals and moral standards related to masculinity and femininity (Attwood, 2007).

## Gaming as a Form of Masculine Sociability

Video gaming is a contemporary activity that – at first glance – seems not to fit in an obvious way into boys' constructions of the gendered binary of masculine physical activity and feminine (passive) talking. Yet, gaming is a very gendered phenomenon and was a central means of doing gender and gender difference in the study. Both quantitative and qualitative studies find that boys are more likely than girls to play digital games. Girls and women do play, but they tend to play on different games and in different ways than boys do. For instance, from a longitudinal Norwegian study of 873 children (boys and girls) followed from age six to 12, Hygen and colleagues (2020) suggested that gender intersects with gaming in different ways for boys and girls:

> [B]ecause studies of gaming, including the current investigation, show that boys spend substantially more time gaming than do girls (...) it could be that gaming is more integrated in boys' play culture and thus plays an important part of boys' socialization. Because girls' gaming is less socially normative, other girls may be less accepting of girls who game a lot. Thus, girls who game may not only have fewer in-person girls to game with, but also to a greater extent be excluded from nongaming social interaction with same-aged girls, and the socialization that follows. (Hygen et al., 2020: 870–71)

This gender difference also intersects with age in that there do not appear to be particular gender differences in gaming among young children, but girls tend to reduce the time they spend gaming from their early teens onwards, while boys increase their playing time

(Livingstone, 2009). In later adolescence, boys have been found to play more frequently than girls do and spend more time on each playing session (Lucas and Sherry, 2004). These differences are not absolute in that some girls play what are often considered to be games liked by boys (Jenson and de Castell, 2011).

In this study, boys spontaneously raised the issue of gaming as a gendered activity. In a focus group interview with two 12-year-old boys, Valtteri reminded Kristian repeatedly that the gender differences related to gaming are not absolute, but are 'usually', and Valtteri himself reported currently gaming much less than previously. Yet, as in almost all interviews, the masculinity of gaming activity was not questioned. It was also clear that it was not using technical devices like computers or phones, or engaging in online activities, that was gendered per se. There is a consensus that social media was an area in which girls were more invested, while gaming was particularly 'a boys' thing'. In the following extract, Kristian spontaneously mentioned that playing video games differentiates girls and boys' activities.

> MP: How about are there the kind of things that, like, girls do some things more and boys do some things?
>
> Valtteri: Yeah generally there are like, boys do some specific things more.
>
> Kristian: Well boys at least play video games.
>
> Valtteri: Usually.
>
> Kristian: Yeah like, girls use these social media services and send pictures of themselves. So that, the video game is a boys' thing.
>
> Valtteri: Usually at least. (*Focus group 4, 2 boys, 12 years, Finnish background, Nurmi School*)

Similarly, in a focus group discussion with four 13-year-old boys, it was recognised that the gender difference in gaming is not absolute. Yet, the contents of many games are considered masculine (shooting, adventure), and, while the boys were aware that several kinds of games exist, gender difference was highlighted in Jaakko's ridiculing of games with more 'feminine' content:

> MP: Well how about, is gaming something that girls and boys do the same way or is it like—
>
> Daniel: Usually men or boys play games. You do see women as well sometimes but not often.
>
> MP: What do you think what is it about that it interests more—?
>
> Daniel: Usually in games they shoot or go on adventures or something really boyish usually.
>
> MP: Mmm, so because of that it doesn't interest girls?
>
> Jaakko: Then there are Barbie make-up games. They are the best adventure games. (*Focus group 3, 4 boys, 13 years, three with Finnish background, one mixed parentage, Nurmi School*)

The area of gaming, then, is one way in which old ideas about gender difference have sedimented into contemporary understandings through practices in new media. Because boys and girls see this as a difference of choice, it is an area in which they feel entitled to essentialise difference, even if they recognise that gender differences should be nuanced.

Online activities and gaming are topics that are often publicly debated with a lot of concern expressed about young people in general and young masculinities in particular, in ways that sometimes come close to being moral panics (Livingstone and Blum-Ross, 2020). Gaming is feared to be addictive; it is thought to interfere with boys' ability to concentrate on schooling or reading, and prevent them from engaging in outdoor activities. The violent material that some of the games contain is thought to be especially harmful (Lobel et al., 2017). The participants in this study were very aware of these concerns. They repeatedly distanced themselves from the problematic notions of 'gaming boys' by stating that they did not play the 'really' violent games and, even if the games had violence in them, they played them for the adventure and tactical strategies they required, not because of the violence:

> Leo: Well I play the kind of adventure games with friends or then when I play, one of these kind of so-called fighting games but really it's not that kind of a fighting game. It is animated and then it is, what makes a fighting game an actual fighting game is that if there is, blood and everything like that but there isn't in this one. So… (*Focus group 2, 2 girls 2 boys, 12–13 years, Finnish background, Nurmi School*)

> MP: What kind of games are the funniest in your opinion or what do you like to play?
>
> Ivan: Online war games, so that with a friend you just go somewhere and then, not for killing but for fun, you know, so that there are different, when there are mistakes and you use the mistakes and all the players are just looking at you, at what are you doing and so it is just fun sometimes. (*Individual interview Ivan, 13 years, Russian background, Harju School*)

The social nature of the gaming – whether online or with a shared device – was also often emphasised. Many of the boys said that playing alone was boring, but multiplayer games were exciting and fun. Playing with a friend was fun because they were able to strategise together and 'compare kills'. In addition, the elements of collaboration, comparison and competition were important as well.

> Veeti: So but it's not the main thing, I just like those type of gameplays more and then I play quite a lot of first person shooting games so.
>
> MP: Yeah, so what does that like mean? So you are the one who shoots?
>
> Veeti: It means that I'm like the dude and then I play against many other players. I like those, I have quite [many], like with Olli, the other friend of mine, [we play] those games always in multiplayer. (…) It's like that it's not traditional

> like run-and-shoot, but rather it's tactic based. (…) I have a lot of games which you can play only- or well like the two of you on a couch and then some games are like that whichever way so you can play them online or then on the couch. (…) I, I like to play with friends, [no matter] if it was online or physically, because you always have more fun in a way that if you share the experience in a way. And then it gets a new dimension as well because you can be in some communication in FPS games, that is in first person shooter games, so you can be with someone else like so hey you go there and get them here and then I shoot them from here. (*Individual interview Veeti, 13 years, Finnish background, Nurmi School*)

The amount of knowledge the boys had about the games and their origins, their detailed narratives on how games are played and the excitement with which gaming was talked about all suggest that gaming is a significant part of everyday social life for most of the boys. However, their expression of enthusiasm was attenuated by their awareness of how problematic the adults considered this activity to be. For instance, in a focus group discussion with five 12-year-old boys, they made clear that it was important to distance themselves from 'playing too much'. Bikram, Mikael and Luka all sought to construct themselves as reasonable players who independently wanted to keep gaming in balance with other (outside) activities and especially football, their hobby. Yet, gaming seemed to have a compelling side for them as well, since Bikram explained that his parents try to limit his gaming when he plays 'well' and both Mikael and Bikram reported sometimes having played until they experienced eye strain or got a headache:

MP: You play a lot? With Playstation?

Luka: No.

Bikram: Yea, not that much.

Mikael: I kind of draw limits.

Bikram: Right there is a limit for example.

Mikael: My mum does not really always need to tell me to put the game away since I can do that myself.

Bikram: And then we have football [training] and such too.

Mikael: Yea so there is not always time.

Bikram: Time and neither does one necessarily want to play. We do not always only go to training, even though we did not have training we would play football, as it is fun and so. (…)

Mikael: They [parents] don't usually, they don't set limits but…

Bikram: But If I play something well then they try to draw limits a bit.

Mikael: Like it's time to go out or something like that.

Luka: We do know how to limit our play time.

MP: So you yourselves know how to.

Bikram: Yea.

Mikael: But my eyes get sore sometimes, if you watch [too long]—

Bikram: And I get a headache if I watch in excess so I draw a limit, [must] stop.

Mikael: I know that before it, it comes so then I know. (*Focus group 6, 5 boys, 12 years, one with Finnish background, two with migrant parents, two mixed parentage, Harju School*)

Despite all the positive aspects the boys knew gaming involved, and despite it being a common social activity for most of them, gaming and especially excessive gaming was also used to draw distinctions between boys. Excessive gaming was seen to be related to geekiness/nerdiness and sometimes even social exclusion. Despite the rise of 'geek chic' (Bell, 2013), in two schools the boys who were especially strongly engaged with gaming were considered to form a group of their own – a group that was not high in the social hierarchy, perhaps because the time they spent gaming took them away from being available for interactions with boys in general.

> Bikram: Well usually the unpopular guys are just those who play quite a lot, I have noticed that they get asked a lot about why they play all the time and so on. And then people do not know them and neither do they care for them and so on. (*Individual interview Bikram, 12 years, Nepalese background, Harju School*)

As a more exceptional case, Sami and Katriina – who were interviewed at a youth club and went to none of the three schools – described 'gamer boys' as an inferior group in schools' masculine hierarchy, based on their less affluent and minoritised ethnic positioning as compared to the white Finnish boys, many of whom were engaged with sports. According to them, the white Finnish boys had the economic (and other) means to enhance their sporting skills, which accorded them high status in the masculine hierarchy; and thus all the other boys, including all boys of other ethnicities, were collapsed together as 'gamer boys' who were considered less masculine.

## Sharing Thoughts and Emotions with Friends

So far, we have seen that (a limited) inclusivity, joking and the importance of fun were an integral part of boys' sociality and friendships. When talking about the school context, the boys often said that all the boys in their class were their 'friends', which fitted with the norms of sociality and masculine inclusivity. Yet, most of them had a more or less stable set of closer friends, with whom they spent time outside, as well as inside, the school context.

When spending leisure time with (male) friends, the boys said that they did sports, played games with computers, hung out in parks, playgrounds and homes, and sometimes went to the cinema, ate hamburgers or shopped. Some boys also explicitly mentioned talking as an activity, usually related to hanging out and having fun. Talking, when it was not joking, however, had a rather marginal position in boys' narratives on their leisure activities. On the whole, the boys' narratives on their friendships followed traditional gendered narratives where boys' friendships centre around common activities and where verbal sharing is seen as 'feminine'.

Stressing the importance of friends did not mean that the friendships would develop to be intimate or confiding. Studies have shown repeatedly that expressions of emotion like hurt, worry and care or concern for others are considered 'gay' or 'girly' and therefore not easily adopted as a part of boys' peer and friendship practices (e.g. Oransky and Marecek, 2009; Way, 2011; Huuki and Sunnari, 2015). Way (2011) described how sharing 'deep thoughts' with friends becomes increasingly difficult for boys as they become adolescents and older, even though they long for such intimate and confiding relationships to last. In the Finnish context, Huuki and Sunnari (Huuki, 2010b; Huuki and Sunnari, 2015) discussed how boys' narratives of caring for and about others gets intertwined with masculine status-seeking and aggression, with the result that generalised empathy towards others may decrease as the boys grow older. For both Way (2011) and Huuki and Sunnari (2015), middle childhood or early adolescence are years of change, during which mechanisms related to masculinity start to interfere with boys' expression of care, worries and 'deep thoughts'. The data from this study also demonstrates that showing emotions and sharing, especially negative emotions and talking about emotions, was not easy and not often done by the boys. Some, like Mikael, explicitly acknowledged that the spectrum of emotions that boys could freely express was very limited: 'Yeah, they [girls] do speak more [about emotions], we [boys] don't really. No, we are never like that, except for maybe the only one there is, is that, "I'm tired". It is the only one. But not really anything else.' However, the narratives were more nuanced than simply rejecting such sharing as feminine. When boys were asked whether they thought the stereotype of 'more emotional' girls was accurate, many of the boys agreed, but some were ambivalent and some rejected the notion:

MP: Sometimes, it's maybe a bit of a stereotype as well that girls were like somehow more emotional or something like that so, do you think that's true?

Samu: Well I don't think it's like in any way, any way true that, I do know boys who are just as emotional as girls and, girls who don't like mind anything like that in a special way. (*Individual interview Samu, 13 years, Finnish background, Nurmi School*)

Many of the boys were critical of the masculine stereotypes of boys being unwilling or unable to express empathy and feelings, in line with the common tendency to question (some) gendered stereotypes and to emphasise gender equality. However, at a practical level, 'talking deep' or sharing one's own worries or negative feelings was not common according to the boys. For instance, Aleksi seems simultaneously to try to reject the masculine stereotype – by claiming his ability to be empathetic and talk with a friend about anything he is struggling with – and to reinforce it by asserting that he prefers doing something fun to having intimate discussions:

MP: What do you think, do boys talk about that [feelings] amongst themselves or, with someone?

Aleksi: I do, for example I might talk with some friend about that if they are going through, a rough time with something or if someone asks for example for some advice, wherever they are so then I kinda talk with them about it but I have never had, myself, a need to talk about deep stuff. I really prefer to do something fun with my friends, than talk about any[thing]. (*Individual interview Aleksi, 12 years, Finnish background, Nurmi School*)

Aleksi shows one of the contradictions that was part of many of the narratives on masculinity. While the boys were willing to question masculine stereotypes and to embrace the multiplicity of masculinities at the level of discourses, when talking about their own practices and everyday lives, they were keen to avoid 'feminine' sharing and showing emotions. Aleksi implicitly denigrates talking about 'deep stuff' by suggesting that he 'prefer[s] to do something fun'. Veeti, who was an exceptionally articulate and reflexive interviewee, engaged in a longer discussion on gender differences in showing negative emotions and especially boys' avoidance of crying:

MP: Maybe a bit like a stereotype as well that girls are somehow more so-called emotional than boys, so do you think that it's true?

Veeti: Well yeah boys show their feelings or talk about it quite rarely, like 'hey I'm having a bit of a hard time' or anything like that.

MP: So in a way it's true.

Veeti: Yeah I think it's probably mostly true, or I don't know if girls reveal to each other like 'hey now I'm upset, this happened', but like boys rarely even try. The thing is more like, if you feel like crying so don't by any means cry if there are friends nearby, so yeah. At least for me it's the kind of thing that I don't want to cry if there are others around.

MP: What is that about, then if someone saw that you were…?

Veeti: Upset or?

MP: Yeah.

Veeti: I don't know, it can… I don't know.

MP: You just get that kind of feeling.

Veeti: Yeah you sometimes even think about it, that 'why?'. But it's quite rare that 'let me just cry', like. With adults or parents I let myself [cry] because it doesn't matter, but then I don't maybe like it if I was for example hurt, so I will try until the last moment to hold back the tears because, maybe it is that, that I don't like at all if everyone looked at you like that like hey something bad happened to that one or something like that. Or if you for example get offended by something so then you are thought to be a bit weak or something like this if you start to cry. (*Individual interview Veeti, 13 years, Finnish background, Nurmi School*)

There is a long tradition of considering crying as particularly antithetical to masculinity. As Veeti's extract shows (above), when crying, one is not necessarily making a decision to share emotions with others, but losing control over tears is an unwelcome deviation from 'rational' and 'controlled' masculinity. It is thus not surprising that, for many boys, crying was an undesired act of showing emotions, which they either avoided or perceived with great ambivalence, as is commonly found in the literature (Motro and Ellis, 2017; Santiago-Menendez and Campbell, 2013).

According to de Boise and Hearn (2017), rather than simply suggesting that boys and men 'repress' their emotions or arguing for the emergence of new and 'more emotional' masculinities, it would be useful to explore how emotions are connected with social structures and how masculine privilege stems from, and is supported through, certain emotions (see also Pease, 2012). Thus, if thinking about Veeti's narrative, rather than simply repressing his emotions when fighting tears, he seemed to be acting in accordance with another emotion – fear and worry about being considered weak or unmasculine – when doing so. Like many other boys, there was an element of critical questioning of the masculine norm for Veeti, yet the costs of being seen crying – being looked at, being considered weak – were clearly too high to make it possible for Veeti to go against the norm in practice. In his short extract, Veeti also illustrated the importance of context, and the plurality of the relationality that constitutes masculinities in relation to being able or unable to show emotions. He regarded crying with adults and especially his parents as unproblematic. His masculine identity as a child ran counter to his school-based masculinity, supporting Tolonen's (2017) argument that practices cannot be divorced from context.

More direct criticism of masculine demands to avoid showing emotions and especially crying is evident in a quote from Liban's interview:

> Liban: I think that, some boys just are like that, that one has to be hard and can't show emotions (…) Because usually, if girls (…) are sad, they usually go to some of their friends. But

then, you don't necessarily have that friend. Then, like, even though you were crying then everybody else would be immediately like, 'Why you are crying? You are a man', like that you know, like 'Yes we know that you feel bad but you don't need to show it'.

MP: Okay I see. So in a way it's, not so easy for boys.

Liban: Maybe, I don't know. But that doesn't apply to me anyway.

MP: Okay so you feel that you have the kind of friends that even if you had something worse going on, you could tell them about that?

Liban: Yeah, but I don't think I ever get those, which is a good thing. (*Individual interview Liban, 14 years, Somali background, Kukkula School*)

According to Liban, 'some boys' had adopted the masculine ideals of hardness and avoiding showing emotions, and these boys were actively sanctioning other boys' expressions of emotion by demanding that they 'man up' if crying. Gendered differences also come up in different social patterns. From Liban's extract, he viewed girls as more often having the kind of close friendships where showing emotions is allowed, while (some) boys generally do not. This corresponds to survey findings in Finland according to which boys and girls meet their friends roughly as often as each other, but boys report getting less emotional support in their friendships and more often report that they have no close friends (Halme et al., 2018; Myllyniemi, 2014). Masculine norms seem to situate boys' friendships more in the public sphere with less close relationships rather than close (male) friendships.

While Liban distanced himself from the masculine demands of hardness and avoiding emotions ('that doesn't apply to me anyway'), it is noteworthy that, when he was asked about whether he would be able to show emotions and share his problems with a friend, he only replied that he did not need to do this. This was a very common pattern in the data. Boys criticise the masculine stereotype and say that it is fine to disrupt them – and yet they represent themselves in ways that resist questioning of the masculine norms in practice. In Liban's case (above), he constructs himself as never having problems, which implicitly constructs himself as strong and autonomous and so normatively masculine.

However, for some boys, close friendships provided a context that allowed at least potential sharing of even some negative emotions and worries. Onni (14 years, Finnish background, Kukkula School), for instance, said that he could speak about his worries with some trusted friends: 'It [that girls share their emotions more than boys] might be quite a bit true, but I can for example tell some of my best friends some things just like that, I know that they don't say anything about it again.' Veeti, on the other hand, speaking again about the difficulties of sharing worries with friends, constructed differences between his friends on the grounds that some are more empathic and better equipped to deal empathically with intimate confiding, while some 'freeze':

> MP: Are there things that you could talk about (…) to your parents but not with friends (…) worries maybe?
>
> Veeti: Yeah worries. Well some worries are after all the kind that your friends can listen to and (…) some friends can but some can't. Some are a bit like… 'I don't know how to answer that' so they freeze completely, but then again some, (…) think about it for a moment and then they start to talk about something to me. So some in a way understand the situation, some are a bit like that they don't really know how I'm feeling. So some are worse at empathy and some are better at empathy. (*Individual interview Veeti, 13 years, Finnish background, Nurmi School*)

The above examples highlight the importance of context, social relations and friendships for boys' potential to share (negative) emotions. Way (2011) argued, based on her long-term longitudinal studies with boys, that, in their childhood, boys enjoy sharing their deepest thoughts and secrets and emotions with their closest friends. While the wish to do so remains even when they grow older, they find it increasingly hard to share the closeness and trust that would enable them to do so. In this study, too, many participants were critical of masculine demands to conceal emotions. Yet, despite their claims to eschew gender differences, they also expressed reluctance to share worries and negative emotions, constructing these as more the domain of girls.

## In Conclusion

In coming back to the theorisation of hegemonic and other masculinities discussed in Chapter 1, via a discussion of boys' relationships with their peers, the boys in the Helsinki schools might be viewed as positioned in processes of change that were visible in contradictory narratives. For example, they espoused egalitarian discourses of gender and sometimes sexuality but reproduced long-standing notions of gender difference in friendships that rendered girls inferior and maintained homophobic name-calling as routine and harmless. This nuancing of masculinities should not be viewed as simply progress from prejudice to egalitarianism but as the ways in which hegemonic masculinities enables the holding of contradictory notions of gender and society in stasis. It suggests that, rather than assuming that one or another 'side' of the debate about homophobia in schools and 'inclusive masculinity' is to be valorised, it is instead crucial to recognise that masculinities among friends and peers are both nuanced and hierarchical. Indeed, de Boise (2014) suggested that practices considered to characterise 'inclusive masculinity' may themselves be one contemporary way in which hegemonic masculinities are flexibly maintained.

The next chapter brings together some of the ideas discussed in this chapter by considering boys' identifications with a range of representations of other boys and men.

CHAPTER 6

# (Dis)identification with Representations of Masculinities

The previous chapters have analysed participants' accounts of how they negotiate masculinities in school with boys, girls and teachers, reproducing old themes of gendered hierarchies and producing newer narratives of gender equality. This study aimed to focus on both boys' narratives and their identifications with other boys and men, with a view to enhancing our insights into the intersections that make a difference to their understandings of masculinities and desires for particular versions of masculinities. To that end, we showed all the participants interviewed individually a range of photographs of boys and men in a photo-elicitation task.

Photo-elicitation involves bringing photographs into the research process so that, rather than depending only on words, the researcher can get at the participants' symbolic representations or their responses to pre-existing symbolic representations. It can help to capture intimate dimensions of social life that may not arise in interviews. Photographs allow both researcher and participant to frame the social world and enable participants to respond to a broader range of objects, people and artefacts than would otherwise be available to them (Harper, 2002). As Clark-Ibáñez (2004) suggested,

> photographs act as a medium of communication between researcher and participant. The photographs do not necessarily

> represent empirical truths or 'reality.' (…) Researchers can use photographs as a tool to expand on questions and simultaneously, participants can use photographs to provide a unique way to communicate dimensions of their lives.

In this study, we were interested in learning about aspects of masculinities that boys might not think of when talking in an interview, but that might be elicited by a visual image. This method has now been used in numerous studies and is particularly favoured in research with children and young people (Cooper, 2017; Frosh et al., 2002; Phoenix et al., 2016).

Many photo-elicitation studies ask participants to take their own photos and use them as triggers to memory and entry points into understanding participants' lives, relations and practices (Croghan et al., 2008). In this study, the aim was to see how the participants engaged with normative and non-normative constructions of masculinities as represented in photographs we presented to them, the stories they told about them and the reasons they gave for liking or disliking particular images. As part of the individual interviews, we presented the participants with 21 photographs of boys and men. The photographs were downloaded from free web-based photograph banks and, in selecting them, we paid attention to different representations of masculinities and tried to include photographs of boys and men of different ages and generations who were differently racialised and seemed to come from different social classes, alone and together with others, and in different contexts (e.g. in nature, doing sports, working, doing childcare). We asked the participants: which photos they liked, which boys or men in the photos they liked or identified with, which they disliked or disidentified with, and whether there were boys or men in the photos whom they considered particularly masculine or unmasculine. We asked them to pick one to three pictures they considered fitted into each of these categories. While photo-elicitation was not a major part of the interview, it gave us important insights into how different masculinities are viewed by the boys and their connotations.

Some of the photographs, or the masculinities featuring in them, were readily accepted by participants, while others attracted relatively little attention from them, and yet others created more contradictory comments, being liked and disliked in equal measure. Generally, the photographs that many interviewees liked tended to represent boys and men in contexts that corresponded with what the boys had already explained that they appreciated or were interested in: being sporty and/or being in friendly relations with other boys (or men). Among the photographs that were often picked as most liked or identified with was a photograph taken of a football field, featuring four white, young boys playing football (see Image 6.1). The other photographs of boys or men engaged in sports (skateboarding, ice hockey) were also relatively popular among the participants and were seldom picked as a disliked image.

While the images that uncontroversially united the boys in liking added substance to their canonical narratives about proper and popular masculinity, the cases where they disagreed helped us to see how masculinities are intersectional and nuanced. Three such cases are worthy of note. The first, a photograph we have entitled 'Friends' (see Image 6.2), features five boys, who are (according

**Image 6.1:** Boys playing football.
Source: Pixabay/joshdick75.

**Image 6.2:** Friends.
Source: Pixabay/AndreCarvalhoFotografia.

to our estimation) some years older than the participants in our study and from mixed minoritised ethnic groups, standing side by side, most of them wearing clothing or accessories that suggest hip-hop culture.

This photograph was picked by 14 participants in their individual interviews. Six identified with one or more of the boys in the photo, and five chose it as their favourite. However, five participants also chose this photo as the one they wanted to disidentify from, or the one they disliked, and two picked it as their least favourite photo. The participants who liked this photo generally liked that the boys looked good-humoured, funny and in friendly relations with each other. For instance, Onni (14 years, white Finnish, Kukkula School) said, 'this photo reminds me a little bit of my own circle of friends' and Mikael (12 years, mixed parentage, Harju School) said that he liked it 'because they are with friends and they look like carefree and happy'.

However, for others, the photograph 'Friends' raised very different associations and the boys in them were described as being 'hard guys' or 'gangsters'. The discussion with Veeti illustrates such connotations, but also the difficulties some of the participants had when they felt that they were expected to 'evaluate' the people in the photos.

MP: For instance, [is there someone] represented in a photo there that you wouldn't like or like that.

Veeti: Well not so hugely, like, I don't know about these people… I find it hard to pass judgment on people immediately, at the first glance.

MP: Of course.

Veeti: I am really bad at evaluating people, like this is this type of a person and that one is of that type. But maybe I would say that someone like this person [points his finger to the boy who is standing second from the right].

MP: This one, in the middle?

Veeti: Yeah. But it's possible that he has for instance, as a joke, done that or so.

MP: What about him makes you think he wouldn't be your type of person?

Veeti: Just because of that I'm not terribly much a person who, like, I don't like hard guys that much, or those who are hard and like that. Only because that I couldn't probably be with them, have anything to do with them or like that, because, I don't know how to be with people like that. (*Individual interview Veeti, 13 years, Finnish background, Nurmi school*)

In a similar way, Eino (14 years, white Finnish, Kukkula School) said that 'I probably wouldn't get along with these guys either. I think they may be some, like hard guys or like that', and Liban (14 years, Somalian background, Kukkula School) briefly stated: 'just because they look like gangsters'. It is noteworthy that neither the boys who liked this photo nor those who disliked it commented upon the boys in the photo being 'people of colour', although racialising stereotypes may play a part in why the boys in the photo appear to some to be 'gangster-like' or 'hard guys'.

Such avoidance may relate to the participants' difficulties in finding vocabularies for discussing racialised difference, combined with the wish to avoid being seen as making racist judgements (see Chapter 8). This tendency, together with the fact that Veeti was a white Finn who very rarely encountered people of other ethnicities in his everyday life, may partly account for Veeti's tentativeness and apparent discomfort at explaining that he did not like the image.

Unlike the others, Sami and Katriina, who were the only participants to do the photo-elicitation task together, said explicitly that it was the boys' version of masculinity in particular that made them dislike the photo:

> Katriina: Well they look like pretty much like the basic dude bros. [Laughs]
>
> Sami: Yeah, a kind of lad atmosphere. (*Focus group 7, a trans boy and a girl, 15 years, Finnish background, Keinu youth club*)

The second photograph that received contradictory comments among the participants was a photo we named 'A crying man' (see Image 6.3). It is a black-and-white photograph of a youngish white man in a suit, crying. The camera angle and focus make the arrangement a little less conventional than most of the other photos.

This photograph was picked by several boys as the one they liked the least or the one they disidentified from. These boys paid attention to the fact that the man was crying, and therefore he was sad; this was something they did not want for themselves. Johannes (13 years, Finnish, Nurmi School), for instance, said that 'basically it depends on why this one is sad, but, generally, like, if there's much negativity, that is what I don't want anyway'. Kasper (13 years, Finnish, Nurmi School) only described the photo as 'weird' and, when asked whether the weirdness was because the man was crying, just repeated, 'Maybe, I don't know. It's just weird.'

However, two boys – Martin and Joel – selected this photograph as their favourite. Both these boys had few friends and were at the

**Image 6.3:** A crying man.
Source: Unsplash / Tom Punford.

margins of their school's masculine hierarchy, possibly because they came from relatively disadvantaged socio-economic positions and did not engage with the loud, joking masculine sociability that was considered central to masculinities by many of the boys. They had quieter communication styles. Besides picking the photo as his favourite, Martin also chose it as the most masculine in the selection, explaining that the man in the photo is doing something that runs counter to what is expected from him: 'Since he is not very well given permission [to cry] or it is, for him it [takes] a lot so if he cries he is masculine 'cause he does something that should not be possible.'

The theme of crying and masculinity is one we discussed more broadly in Chapter 5, where we showed that the long tradition of understanding crying as 'unmasculine' still has power over the boys, although they also critiqued this idea. Martin was one of the interviewees who initiated a discussion on this topic in the focus group, where he explained that his mother expected him to be 'like a brick', that is, to avoid expressing emotions. He made clear that he disagreed with this idea. It is therefore likely that this issue felt particularly compelling to him. By choosing the picture as his favourite, he is likely to have been resisting his mother's strictures as well as picking the representation of a man he considered also resisted what he saw as the curtailment of men's emotional freedom.

The third photograph discussed here as one which raised contradictory responses among the study participants, is a photo of a black man, wearing heart-shaped sunglasses and a pink cap, hugging the back of a bearded man and being hugged by a curly-headed man wearing his heart-shaped sunglasses on the back of his head (see Image 6.4). It therefore represents the intersection of racialisation, gender and probably sexuality.

This photograph was picked by some of the boys as featuring someone who is 'unmanly' or 'untypical' for a man. Bikram explained that the 'unmanliness' in the photo came simply from a man hugging another man:

> MP: What is it [the unmanly deed] here?
>
> Bikram: Well that he hugs another man or like that. Well I haven't talked to them so I cannot really say but. (*Individual*

**Image 6.4:** A man with heart-shaped sunglasses.

Source: Unsplash / Dimitar Belchev.

*interview Bikram, 12 years, Nepalese background, Harju School*)

Not all of the participants who considered hugging 'unmanly' explicitly connected hugging with intimate interest in another man, and thus homosexuality, but this interpretation also featured in reasons for considering this photograph 'unmanly': 'This photo somehow (…) like it might be just that [he is] interested in other boys, it is possible, I don't know' (Onni, 14 years, Finnish background, Kukkula School).

Understanding homosexuality as 'unmasculine' is in line with how calling someone 'gay' was still used as a way to police ways of being masculine among boys. Illustrative of the contradictions within the data, many participants expressed a degree of acceptance towards actual homosexual people, while still using the term 'gay' 'jokingly' but in an insulting way with their peers (see Chapter 5). The combination of a wish to express oneself as accepting homosexuality in other people and the simultaneous desire to be seen as detached from it is also present in Elias's (14 years, Finnish background, Nurmi School) explanation of why he chose it as both 'unmanly' and the one he disidentified with: 'Somehow this photo is, in the sense that I wouldn't like to be there myself but whatever, I don't mind if they are there or not.' So, even as Elias explains his dislike of the photo, he is careful to couch this in a way that expresses tolerance of behaviour he would not like for himself.

However, there were also some participants who particularly liked this photo. For instance, Samu, while also referring to the possible homosexuality of the two men, considered that the photo includes happiness and freedom to be oneself in a way that he likes:

> Samu: I don't know if there is a hint that he was, that the guy was gay but I, or I don't know, when it's like that, he hugs men and I thought that if that's something, a Pride parade or like that. But I mean, they appear being very happy and the way, like, that he understands everybody and lets everybody to be as they are. (*Individual interview Samu, 13 years, Finnish background, Nurmi School*)

Identifying with a photo that aroused homosexual connotations is likely to demand a degree of self-confidence and courage, even if a boy is simultaneously distancing himself from homosexuality, given the long tradition of homophobia in schools. Samu indeed showed a great deal of self-confidence throughout the interview (and even before it, being the first in his school to show interest in, and willingness to, participate in the study). Furthermore, he seemed to have a secure position in the school's masculine hierarchy – he had many friends and was also one of the very few boys who told the interviewer that they currently had a girlfriend. All these characteristics may have facilitated his confidence in choosing this image. This photo was also immediately picked as a favourite by Katriina and Sami, both of whom talked extensively about their queer identities in their joint interview. Neither of them considered markers of hegemonic masculinity attractive or worth seeking; both had also clearly thought carefully about their own gendered identities and gender more broadly. They expressed themselves fluently on these points. As with Martin's response to the photo of the crying man, it is noteworthy that Katriina considered this man to be particularly 'manly', on the grounds that he was secure enough about his masculinity to be able to hug another man:

> Katriina: But, I'd almost say that those guys hugging here [are the most manly], because, for the greater part, men don't hug each other just because they are a bit insecure about their own masculinity and identity. Like, these guys clearly are confident about what they are and they don't mind starting to hug each other, so that is it in my opinion. (*Focus group 7, a trans boy and a girl, 15 years, Finnish background, Keinu youth club*)

This third more 'controversial' photo also did not prompt any discussion related to racialisation, although the central character in the photo is black. Besides the difficulties many of the young people had in discussing racialisation (discussed in Chapter 8), this may possibly be because the sexuality hinted at in the representation preoccupied the participants in their reflections, attracting some and repelling others.

The photo-elicitation method proved an illuminating addition to the interview accounts, allowing us to explore from a different vantage point, the subjective meanings they attached to particular photos and their thinking about them (Croghan et al., 2008). The photographs did, as many researchers have argued, evoke complex emotions in some cases that helped us to understand more about dominant notions of masculinities and the points at which the boys resisted various versions of masculinities. They helped us to nuance our versions of masculinities, gave us hints about intersectional engagement with versions of masculinities and identity issues in terms of boys' claims to egalitarian discourses, even as they made clear that they eschewed some versions of masculinities for themselves. The polarised accounts of likes and dislikes for some images were particularly helpful in this process, extending our understanding of boys' meaning-making processes. As Luttrell (2020: vi) suggested, they gave us 'an appreciation for the layered meanings and intentions' that they produced.

## In Conclusion

Bringing focus groups, individual interviews and photo-elicitation together helped us to see that the participants were differentiated according to the elements of masculinities they liked. Given the apparent consensus about many aspects of masculinities at school, the photo-elicitation enabled valuable nuancing as well as giving us insights into the intersections of masculinities with racialisation, sexuality, age and social class.

The chapter that follows considers boys' narratives about their relations at home. It addresses the question of whether boys are able to maintain close relations at home, with family members, in ways that are less available to them at school and in their hobbies.

CHAPTER 7

# Family Relationships

The chapters above have discussed the ways in which masculinities can only be understood relationally and are crafted in relation to other boys (and men) and to girls (and women) (Connell, 1995). As shown in Chapter 3, boys in the pre-teen and early teenage years recognise that they behave differently when with boys than on the rare occasions when they spend time with girls. They constantly compare themselves with girls as well as with other boys (Way, 2011).

While boys 'do' masculinity with their peers in school and in their out-of-school activities (as discussed in Chapters 4 and 5), they also spend a great deal of time with one or both parents and, for those who have them, with their siblings, practising masculinity in relation to them. In their London-based study, Frosh, Phoenix and Pattman (2002) found that boys tended to think of their mothers as trustworthy, the person they could confide in if they had to, but someone who was boring and responsible. In contrast, they tended to see their fathers as good fun, sporty and boyish, but not trustworthy because they did not treat confidences seriously. Parenting practices also impact on children's gendered identities and practices (Mesman and Groeneveld, 2018). It is, therefore, important to know how boys experience their parents' gender practices in order to get a nuanced picture of boys' masculinities and family relationships.

Aapola's (1999) analysis of Finnish school textbooks and textual material utilised by family professionals showed that, as in many other countries, 'adolescence' is generally constructed as a problem-oriented life phase characterised by emotional turbulence, desires for greater independence, distancing from parents and inclination to engage in conflict with them. It is certainly a time for reorganising intergenerational relations. The school climate strikes and other collective climate change action for young people have illuminated ways in which young people can aim to do things differently from their parents' generation. It is noteworthy that, alongside changes in their social relations, young people generally continue to consider family and parents central to their well-being (Turtiainen et al., 2007) and to feel loyal towards them (e.g. Peltola, 2018). In studies of adult men, it is the home sphere where, to some extent, caring becomes a possible element of masculine identities, especially through practices of fatherhood (e.g. Eerola, 2014; Eerola and Huttunen, 2011) – in accordance with 'caring masculinities', suggested by Elliott (2016). With the shifts in working patterns impelled by the COVID-19 adjustments, there are suggestions that a minority of men are doing more childcare than previously – although far from equal with mothers (Sevilla and Smith, 2020). Given this potential shift in gender relations at home, it is important to understand how boys consider that they do masculinities at home, rather than school. While this study was conducted before the COVID-19 pandemic, it contributes to the sparse literature on masculinities at home.

This chapter draws predominantly on the individual interviews to present the story of boys' relationships with their mothers and fathers and with their siblings, mostly as told from the boys' perspectives (with a few girls' accounts also discussed). It is striking that most boys in this study told of harmonious relationships with their parents, particularly their mothers, and often with siblings. A few reported particularly close relationships with their mothers. As Turtiainen et al. (2007) found, family and friends were both often named as the most important features of the boys' lives. The chapter first considers boys' narratives of their relationships with their mothers and their fathers, then considers whether they report themselves to be open with their parents about what they are thinking of, what they do and whether or not they confide issues they consider private to their parents. The final main section considers their relationships with their siblings.

## Relationships with Mothers and Fathers

The participants in this study told of many shared activities with their parents and/or their families. These included: travelling, bowling, playing billiards, going to movies and picnics, and just staying at home together with their parents and siblings, cooking, watching TV and playing board and computer games. While some said that spending time with friends was more important for them than spending time with family, almost all seemed to enjoy and appreciate time spent with their families (see also Armila, Käyhkö and Pöysä, 2018; Turtiainen et al., 2007).

Of the 32 participants, 18 lived with both their parents. Among those whose parents had separated, it was more common for the children to live with mothers (and mothers' partners where relevant) and visit fathers who lived separately, even if infrequently. Five considered that they had two homes that they split their time between. Different living arrangements after parental separation – whether having two homes or meeting their fathers frequently or infrequently – were by and large discussed as commonplace and represented as unproblematic.

While relationships with both mothers and fathers were generally considered well-functioning and close, the relationships they reported were highly gendered. Such patterns of gendered parenthood have also been reported by Armila, Käyhkö and Pöysä (2018) in their study of teenage boys living in rural Finland, where this was highlighted when the participants discussed the activities they did with their parents. It was common for the boys in our study, too, to report that they did sports, played games or engaged with other outside activities with their fathers and practised cooking, doing household chores and homework with their mothers.

MP: Do you have some things that you do with your parents, like together in your free time?

Aleksi: Nothing like special. Quite basic, what I now sometimes cook with mum for example. And then with my dad I go to do sports just to play some basketball or floorball, or things like that quite a lot. (*Individual interview Aleksi, 12 years, Finnish background, Nurmi School*)

Boys also explained that they talked about different things with their mothers and fathers. Eino, for example, explained:

MP: What about your dad, do you talk with him about your own things?

Eino: To some extent. When we see. I talk with my dad also quite a lot about games and cars and like, these information technology related things. (...)

MP: Are they somehow different the things, is it easier to speak about some things to your mum or to your dad or?

Eino: Well I mean I never speak with my mother about any car-related things or like that. (*Individual interview Eino, 14 years, Finnish background, Kukkula School*)

Finnish studies indicate that Finnish fatherhood is increasingly active and emotionally engaged (e.g. Eerola and Huttunen, 2011), fitting generally with Finnish norms and ideals of gender equality. While this was also the case in this study, it seems that fathers engaged more in 'masculine' activities outside the home with their sons while mothers engaged with them more in the home, where nurturing, household chores and education were often the focus. The boys' relationships with their fathers thus seem to follow the same pattern of masculine sociality as their relationships with their friends, where 'doing' is preferred to sharing (as in Way, 2011 and Chapter 5). In some cases, such gendered relationships also meant that the role of mothers was seen through the ungratifying activities of repetitive scolding and 'commanding', contrasted with the more 'fun' and carefree activities they engaged in with their fathers (see also Armila, Käyhkö and Pöysä, 2018; Frosh et al., 2002). In the extract below, from a mixed-gender focus group, Leo develops this theme, which Elsa, a girl, co-constructs and extends:

Leo: Well I don't fight, sometimes I argue with my dad but sometimes, or well quite often with my mum. For example this morning. [laughing]

MP: What did you argue about?

Leo: About that, that my mum puts my clothes in the wrong wardrobe. [laughing] (…) But then when my dad puts them into the wrong wardrobe then I just put them back. I don't know. I just [hate] my mum. Or well.

MP: She somehow annoys [you].

Leo: Mum annoys me easier than dad.

Elsa: My mum is really overprotective. She always just complains if I do something and [laughing] then, with my dad we just have fun and go to the cinema, everywhere with my dad and mum is just the person who commands you at home. (*Focus group 2, 2 boys 2 girls, 12–13 years, Finnish background, Nurmi School*)

Two boys, Ivan and Joel, were exceptional in the study in that they reported having particularly close relationships with their mothers. Ivan explained:

MP: How, about your mother then so, how would you say, do you have close relations or are you close with her?

Ivan: Yes, really. I love her and, we are quite– When she can, we are together so that if she's not working a lot. (…) we go to cinema sometimes, visit to [the mall], anything, for example, to a Chinese restaurant where we eat, different places. Like, sometimes we are just at home watching a film, it's quite nice.

MP: Right. Is your mother that kind of person that you, or do you speak also about your own things a lot with her? (…) Is it just easy for example [to talk] about some worries if there are some worries? (…)

Ivan: Well I tell her every time if something happens or so on, just freely I mean, we speak all the time like that.

MP: There are not any kinds of things that you wouldn't tell your mother or is there?

Ivan: No there isn't, we are very close. (*Individual interview Ivan, 13 years, Russian background, Harju School*)

Ivan and Joel were very different in many ways, but they shared some characteristics. They both lived only with their mothers and met their fathers infrequently. Both had experienced social and financial difficulties that may have strengthened their feelings of loyalty and reciprocity in their relationships with their mothers. They also both seemed to have few close friends, if any, with whom to spend time outside school. It seems thus that mothers could potentially still constitute enjoyable company for boys of this age and might be able to compensate for some of their sons' feelings of loneliness when they have relatively few friends.

While parents generally were not described as role models for the participants, there were specific cases where their role was particularly important. In a focus group discussion with a trans boy and his close female friend, the fact that one of their mothers was trans was significant for both participants and was described as a factor that helped them to understand their own identities and the role of gender and sexuality in society more broadly:

Katriina: I have a transgender mother, who came out when I was nine maybe. And then I was like a bit, I went at ten years old probably to the first Pride [event] where I was and then I started to think from that. And then we moved here in Helsinki and I met him [Sami] and introduced him to this lovely rainbow world. (…) It did not in my opinion at least at first seem anyway a terribly big thing, and then things happened and… that yes it was sometimes a bit like that I thought that what is going on here now. But luckily my mother is quite a person that ze is very patient with us and then wanted to explain things to us so, yes then it normalized quite quickly. (…)

Sami: [Before meeting Katriina and her family] I got to know a bit about transgender issues [but] I did not even then, it somehow seemed, the people you probably know. I always saw it just in some strange documents and sometimes heard about the people who want to be women and men who wear women's clothes so that, it was very strange to me so that it was not related to me in any way. Then I met her mother, a nice person, a great person in fact, and it started normalizing a bit and I started to think a bit that what if this could be what I feel, but it still took three years for me until I admitted it to myself and then another half a year until I admitted it also to her [the friend]. (*Focus group 7, a girl and a trans boy, 15 years, Finnish background, Keinu youth club*)

For Sami, it was both that Katriina's transgender mother embodied and normalised trans identities in a way he had not previously experienced and could relate to. In a parallel way, the mothers of the two boys who talked about their mothers as if they were best friends also provided something lacking in the rest of their lives: a close companionate relationship.

## Adolescence and (Diminishing) Parental Authority

Some of the participants described significant changes in their relationships as they grew older. These changes were related to their relations both with their friends and with their parents. Their narratives often highlighted the growing importance of friends and greater independence from parents, which also manifested in an ability to question parental authority to some extent.

For instance, Elias emphasised the transition from primary school to lower secondary school as a threshold that had transformed 'his life'. He now spent more time with his friends than with his parents, a change that also seemed to be connected to his increased popularity at school:

> Elias: I, for example in primary school, I was the kind of person who not many knew. Now that I've come to the 7th grade then suddenly I, most people know me. I don't know why. I think I am pretty much the same as when I was in the sixth grade but. Totally different life anyways.
>
> MP: So it has, changed a lot here?
>
> Elias: Yea. Before I rather spent time at home more than with my friends. Nowadays I rather spend my time outside, sit with friends rather than at home. (*Individual interview Elias, 13 years, Finnish background, Nurmi School*)

Johannes, for his part, emphasised how, nowadays, he wished to distance himself from his parents to some extent and how he 'dared' to do things that might question some of the rules set by his parents. When discussing the areas in the city he had explored, he explained:

> MP: Is there something that you'd do for instance only with your dad or only with your mom?
>
> Johannes: Not really I don't have anything because, it is what in this age it is. One wants a bit to work oneself loose from parents, as it is at this age. (…) When I was little I didn't really, dare to do anything. Nowadays I have more courage but I do know what is reasonable and what is not.
>
> MP: Like what kind of things didn't you dare to do?
>
> Johannes: I didn't really dare to do like, anything that in a way was wrong. Now I dare to resist a bit, but within reasonable limits. And it is so, as it is the part of this age that, in a way it is like 'terrible twos' once again, but a bit, however, different.
>
> MP: Like searching for your own ways to do things and like that?

Johannes: Because when I was in the 3rd grade I really didn't, like, anything… [laughs] I was a very obedient schoolboy. But it's not that I would now want to behave very badly at home. (*Individual interview Johannes, 13 years, Finnish background, Nurmi School*)

Johannes interpreted this change as part of adolescence and, as such, something that is even expected of him. In doing so he borrowed adult psychological vocabulary ('basically this is the terrible twos again'). In his narrative of 'rebellion', responsibility and loyalty have a continued role: he is clear about remaining within reasonable limits and avoiding causing unnecessary difficulty for his parents by not behaving 'very badly at home'.

The participants were also asked about the restrictions and limits set by their parents. On the whole, the boys were approving of parental authority used to set curfews and limits concerning gaming and phone use. These were largely viewed as reasonable. In a mixed-gender focus group Leo, Veeti and Sofia co-constructed a narrative that their parents would not let them see movies that are too violent or too scary. They did not consider that this meant that their parents were 'strict' because they agreed with them:

MP: How strict are your parents, if you think for example about films?

Several respondents [unclear]: Not really…

Leo: Well, they are like if it is, too real, if there are fighting scenes then if it's too authentic so then, no. I'm not allowed to watch anything like that. But in principle I am allowed to watch some K16 films [films rated as suitable for 16-year-olds and older] but, K18 films like they aren't even that good.

Veeti: I have quite the same. (…) My parents trust that I know myself, that if I want to watch them. So if there is for example some crude violence so then, I quite often know how it feels like myself, or that it stays on my mind, for example that in the night I can't sleep, so I do know that generally myself.

Sofia: It's the same for me, so if there is something really brutal or something like that, and then for example in horror films then no, it, you know yourself if you're able to, stand to watch it or if it stays with you because even now if I go to see too young, films for older people, or then some scary ones then it might stay in your brain forever the, film and like that. (*Focus group 2, 2 boys 2 girls, 12–13 years, Finnish background, Nurmi School*)

What is important in the above extract is that the three young people who talked agreed that their parents trusted them and made the restrictions they impose a matter of self-disciplining based on 'knowing themselves' from past experience, rather than external, parental constraint. It is possible that they did not wish the focus group to see them as too restricted by their parents. It may also be, however, that, as Foucault (1977) suggested, disciplinary practices become internalised and so viewed as self-imposed.

In keeping with this, 14-year-old Liban did not question his mother's right to restrict his gaming time so that he had time for other activities. He also explained how he was able to modify the limits set by his mother through negotiation, which highlights his own active role in decisions affecting his everyday life, but also that he viewed his mother's parenting practices as reasonable (Peltola et al., 2017):

MP: If you think for example of social media or those movies or playing or something so are they the kinds of things that, do you have some rules on what you're allowed to do or how much you're allowed to do?

Liban: Yes for example I probably wouldn't be allowed to be on PlayStation for the whole day. That at some point there you should read, then you have to be outside as well and so.

MP: Yes. Is it so that, do you still usually decide yourself then that how much that?

Liban: No, probably mum usually however. [laughs]

MP: She says that now you have been playing enough?

Liban: Yes, but yes I can usually like negotiate for example that if mum is like, 'today you play 30 minutes', for example 'now you play 30 minutes then you have to read and then you can maybe later play a bit more'. So then I'm like ok, 'is it ok if I read a bit more that I play 45 minutes or an hour?' Then she is like ok. (*Individual interview Liban, 14 years, Somali background, Kukkula School*)

Some of the participants seemed to have internalised and adopted the reasons given by their parents on such limitations so well that they used them in the interview as self-evident facts:

Kristian: It is the phone, the important, the most important… part of life, could one say, but all the time I try to use it as little as possible.

MP: Yeah, why do you think that you should use it as little as possible?

Kristian: Well, it is unhealthy for your neck muscles and, you should spend time reading and not watch videos. So it's not, you get that radiation into your eyes and all these problems. Of course I could ask my mum a bit more about the reasons why that is but.

MP: Oh so it is, like that your, have your parents said that, you shouldn't be [on it] so much?

Kristian: Yeah I have been told [that]. (*Focus group 4, 2 boys, 12 years, Finnish background, Nurmi School*)

It is also the case, therefore, that, as in Kristian's narrative above, things that parents say had become part of the young people's own narratives, to the extent that Kristian's account sounds like heteroglossia, with somebody else's words being embodied and delivered by the young people (Bakhtin, 1994; Maybin, 2013).

By and large, then, parental guidance was not much questioned but seen as reasonable and necessary. Many participants also seemed to discuss and negotiate with their parents the reasons behind the limits set for them. The interviews suggest that 'concerted cultivation' (Lareau, 2003) was a widespread parental practice in the participants' families, with parents aiming to maximise the range and quality of children's activities while protecting their health and academic attainment. This was a widely shared feature in all three schools, although social class made a difference to the sort of activities parents were reported to offer to the participants. For instance, parents at Nurmi School were able to offer their children a wider range of and more expensive extracurricular hobbies than parents of participants from the other two schools (see Chapter 2). In addition, the children appeared to have internalised their parents' regulatory narratives in that they reproduced and justified their parents' arguments.

## Sharing Thoughts with Parents

One of the canonical narratives in the study was that the boys had relatively unproblematic and close family relationships. This did not mean, however, that the boys would confide in their parents, telling them what they were thinking and giving them details about their everyday lives. An extract from an interview with 14-year-old Onni summarises well many participants' narratives about talking to parents. While Onni had just said that it was an important aim for the whole family to have dinner together every day, he indicated that his verbal communication with them was based mostly on reacting to his parents' questions, and did not include a self-initiated wish to share his thoughts or give accounts of what he did away from home:

MP: Do you talk a lot with your parents, for example about your school or something like that, do they ask—?

Onni: They always ask what happened at school but I don't really say much, anything, special.

MP: Is it more that they ask and then you answer when you have to [laughs]?

Onni: Yes. I don't really talk about anything special with them.

MP: What if you had sometimes some worries, do you think that, would it be just easy to speak about those with them?

Onni: Yes, I don't have any problem to talk about. (*Individual interview Onni, 14 years, Finnish background, Kukkula School*)

The picture Onni gave is of being deliberately reserved with his parents and so lacking spontaneity, even though he felt that he could talk to them if he wished. Just as many boys indicated that they did not have anything they needed to talk to their friends about (Chapter 5), so Onni and other boys said that they generally did not have anything they needed to discuss with their parents.

In earlier studies, it was suggested that young people, and particularly boys, tend to perceive their families as important resources that they can take for granted will support them if necessary, but that they do not necessarily have to engage with (O'Connor et al., 2004; Turtiainen et al., 2007). As COVID-19 made clear, this only applies to those young people who have safe and relatively unproblematic relationships with their family members. For young people in more difficult family circumstances, there are fewer possibilities for such taken-for-grantedness, even though their families are also important to them (e.g. Wilson et al., 2012). However, the boys' mundane ways of talking about family also highlight the persistent ideals attached to family and the importance of family as an (imagined) community of belonging (Ribbens McCarthy, 2012). The tendency to treat family as a taken-for-granted emotional resource was evident in the current study. For instance, while Onni, above, avoided representing himself as someone who had worries to share, he considered it self-evident that his parents would be interested in his problems and would be there to listen to him should he have any worries that he needed to share.

The reluctance to share details of one's everyday life outside the home with one's parents can be understood as connected to the temporal changes in adolescence discussed above, especially the growing importance given to friendships, loyalty to friends and the boys' anxieties about their positioning among friends. Given that social relationships are an inseparable part of school life, leisure and hobbies, sharing details with their parents would run the risk of sharing things that would implicate their friends and reveal things the friends would prefer not to be known by adults, and particularly parents. According to the participants, this would compromise their loyalty to their friends and their friends' privacy. For instance, Aleksi reported telling his parents 'approximately' what happened in school, while avoiding anything of special significance. Friends' girlfriends and rule-breaking were repeatedly cited as specific examples of things that were not shared with parents.

MP: What kind of things are they then that you talk about with your parents?

Aleksi: Something like, if, usually they ask how has it been in school so then I reply, like, approximately what has happened. I don't now of course if there has been for example, some bigger thing or something, so I don't like necessarily tell that, because then it might become a bigger deal. And my friends don't want that, in a way, that anyone's parents know everything what they are up to. Especially if they don't know them very well.

MP: What kind of things are they then that you don't tell parents?

Aleksi: Exactly something what my friends for example, if someone has a girlfriend then I don't talk about that to my parents. I don't know how they would react but in a way it's not their business so. (*Individual interview Aleksi, 12 years, Finnish background, Nurmi School*)

This observation draws attention to the fact that relationships with parents and relationships with friends do not exist in a vacuum but are interconnected (Castrén and Ketokivi, 2015). The feeling of closeness in relationships with parents does not (necessarily) vanish. However, the possibilities for boys' intimate sharing of the details of their everyday lives with their parents seems to diminish as the importance of friends, loyalty to friends and concern about positioning among friends increases. What is also significant is that masculine norms do not diminish possibilities for the boys to share their thoughts and worries only in one particular site, such as among friends or at home, but do so simultaneously in both these social spheres (see Chapter 5).

Despite the boys' stated reluctance to share confidences with their parents, being able to do so retained some of its (emotional) importance. Elias's contradictory narrative below is one example of this. Elias had earlier stated that he did not really talk with his parents anymore, since it was now more important for him to be with his friends and talk to them.

> MP: You said you don't much talk with them [parents] but are there things you don't tell them, like secrets?
>
> Elias: Definitely there are some things. I myself have a thing that like if I break something, I do think sometimes for a moment that I'd just keep it a secret. Tell them one day. Then I do tell them quite soon after 'cause then I'd forget it if I didn't tell them immediately.
>
> MP: Is it important to tell about those kind of things anyway?
>
> Elias: Yea it is. If I keep it in my mind it's going to stay there. (*Individual interview Elias, 13 years, Finnish background, Nurmi School*)

In the above extract, Elias started by saying that he 'definitely' kept some secrets from his parents but went on to describe a potential situation ('if I break something') that he would talk about with his parents, contrary to his initial idea of keeping it secret. The reason for sharing things that have happened with his parents seems to be the wish to unburden himself of the emotional burden that Elias anticipated he would feel if he did not share such events.

In the previous section we discussed how the boys' relationships with their parents and the activities they engaged in with their parents were gendered. Several participants considered it easier to talk about their own issues – especially worries – with their mothers, while discussion topics with their fathers were often related to hobbies and activities. While, for some, more confiding relationships with mothers were related simply to living with their mothers and meeting their fathers more seldom, this observation was also common among those participants who lived with both their parents. For instance, Veeti, who lived with both his parents, said, 'Well with dad [I talk about] some normal things like for example about some of my interests and like that but with mum it's probably a bit better to talk about worries and so forth.' Often it was not that the boys wanted to keep their fathers ignorant about their lives, worries and ideas but that it felt easier to talk with mothers:

MP: Do you talk about your stuff with your parents a lot, school or some friends or hob—?

Bikram: Yea hobbies, friends... Yea.

MP: Have you ever noticed that there would be any difference, like that it would be easier to discuss certain things with like your mum and some other things with your dad, are there any?

Bikram: No, usually I tell everything to mum.

MP: Is it that it is easier to speak to your mum for some reason?

Bikram: Yea somehow, I don't know... No I do tell my dad but I just prefer telling my mother more and so on.

MP: Yea like somehow it feels easier?

Bikram: Yea. Sure my mum always tells [to dad] and so on, but then to my mother it is easier to tell and so on. (*Individual interview Bikram, 12 years, Nepalese background, Harju School*)

This gendered parental difference has been repeatedly found in earlier studies on boys and masculinities (Frosh et al., 2002; Way, 2011) and is in line with normative notions that emotions are 'feminine' (e.g. de Boise and Hearn, 2017; Chapter 5). The boys' experience about which parent is easier to confide in may, at least partly, be related to the parenting practices they had experienced.

MP: What about have you noticed that there are, for example, some things it would be easier to speak with your mother about, or some things that are easier to speak with your father about? Is there any difference?

Yonas: Yes. Maybe it's easier to speak to my father in my opinion. At least for me.

MP: Do you know why that is, or is it just about personality or something?

Yonas: Well I don't know, maybe. Maybe it's just more that, I can't really, I guess it might be because my father is more, he spends more time with us and so it might be because of that.

MP: He spends more time at home?

Yonas: Yes. No I mean he spends more [time], like with us, the children. (*Individual interview Yonas, 14 years, Eritrean background, Kukkula School*)

Yonas was the only participant in the study who considered it easier to talk to his father than his mother. In this case it was not simply a case of which parent spent more time at home, but that his father spent more time (presumably 'quality time') with his children, including Yonas. However, many of the other boys, too, reported having active and engaged fathers with whom they spent time – in line with recent studies on fatherhood (e.g. Eerola and Huttunen, 2011). Elliott (2016) argued that, in order for 'caring masculinities' to start to evolve, it does not matter whether fathers *care about* (engage in the practical tasks of caring) or *care for* (including affective relations of care), since the former leads to the latter developing. While this seems a plausible argument, our findings suggest that fathers engaging in activities with their sons does not in itself seem to be enough to disrupt the uneasy relationship between masculinities and confiding and lead to the sort of 'caring masculinities' where emotions would be not only lived but also verbally shared between fathers and sons.

## Relationships with Siblings

In addition to relationships with parents, sibling relationships have increasingly been recognised as significant for young people's well-being, identifications and resources (e.g. Davies, 2015; Edwards et al., 2006; Gillies and Lucey, 2006). These intragenerational relationships are not simply, or necessarily, about competing for parental attention but also provide important mutual social resources within and outside their families that help young people to cope with the demands of growing up and becoming adult (Gillies and Lucey, 2006). They also help them to construct their identities in relation to how similar/different they are from their siblings (Davies, 2015). As we saw in Chapter 3, for some boys, sisters gave them an invaluable insight into girls' worlds, even if they professed not to understand girls very deeply.

Only three participants did not have any siblings. Just over half lived in families with two children; however, bigger families were not uncommon, especially in cases where the participants' parents were divorced and re-partnered. Here, stepsiblings and birth siblings were all similarly referred to by the participants as siblings. Most lived with their siblings, but there were some who had siblings who were living elsewhere (part time or full time), either because older siblings were already living independently or because of their parents' separate living arrangements. Tables 6.1 and 6.2 below summarise the number and gender of siblings the participants talked about. In two cases, a participant in a focus group discussion referred to their siblings as a group and did not

**Table 6.1:** Number of siblings reported by participants.

| Number of siblings | Number of participants |
|---|---|
| 0 | 3 |
| 1 | 18 |
| 2 | 4 |
| 3 | 2 |
| 4+ | 5 |

**Table 6.2:** Gender of siblings reported by participants.

| Gender of siblings | Number of siblings |
|---|---|
| Boy | 26 |
| Girl | 24 |
| Not stated | 8 |

specify their genders (these were participants who had several siblings), and therefore this information is not known in all cases.

As was the case with how they talked about their relationships with their parents, most of the participants reported good, or at least unproblematic, relationships with their siblings. Many recounted activities that they did together with their siblings, like playing board and computer games, 'wrestling', watching films and shopping. In keeping with the findings of Edwards and colleagues (2006), and parallel to the gendered activities engaged in with parents, 'doing things together' was more important to reported feelings of closeness and enjoying each other's company than talking or sharing thoughts.

Daniel: [I have a] little brother.

MP: How old is he?

Daniel: Eight.

MP: Okay, right. How do you get along?

Daniel: Good good, we play video games and wrestle and so on. (*Individual interview Daniel, 13 years, mixed parentage, Nurmi School*)

Mikael: With my brother, we both are engaged in, like my big brother, who is my stepbrother, he does badminton and me, football, but then our common thing, like, is airsofting, so that we both have weapons and that. And with my sister, shoes. Yeah, so that what kinds and, cool clothes and like this. And then with my little brother well he is so small that he doesn't really have interests yet, except for Lego, and yeah even me I like to, always when, if he

> gets a new Lego box so it is usually me who builds it for him, since he cannot yet, he is only three years. (*Individual interview Mikael, 12 years, mixed parentage, Harju School*)

However, there also seemed to be more room for contradictory and negative feelings in narratives of sibling relationships than with parents. For boys, this was particularly the case with little sisters, who were repeatedly described as 'annoying' (see also Edwards et al., 2005), but all siblings could enrage or upset young people.

> MP: How about with your little sister?
>
> Kristian: Well they are really, can be quite annoying creatures. So, like, she sometimes gets tantrums out of nothing even though I haven't done anything and, like, a bit… Every now and then they are quite good people but sometimes they are just like the new lows, of a good personality. (…) She has kicked me in the head and then I, have gotten angry and then she goes to tell [parents], 'Kristian hit me,' and then, she of course doesn't say anything about that she has kicked me in the head and I haven't done anything. They happen to be like that. (*Focus group 4, 2 boys, 12 years, Finnish background, Nurmi School*)

> Sami: Ok, my little brother. We have, since we were small, we have been hanging around together a lot so my little brother, we actually both (…) my little brother very quickly learnt how to push my buttons so that I get into a rage and almost cry. (…) That sounds quite awful and it was quite awful. So we had a terrible number of fights, even physical fights. And then we even, we have these frustrating things in our life and we vented them sometimes to each other. But I can say that we have both matured over that, that now we still irritate each other [laughs], like when I steal his headphones when I have lost my own and then he still, I don't know what all he does… a bit of everything. (*Focus group 7, a girl and a trans boy, 15 years, Finnish background, Keinu youth club*)

Despite irritations such as those in the extracts above, the participants who had younger siblings also assumed (some) care responsibilities for them, like helping them with their homework. Many reported that they often enjoyed the role of the responsible big brother. This is in line with Huuki and Sunnari's (2015) finding that, while boys grow increasingly reluctant to show their vulnerabilities, caring and compassion when moving from middle childhood to adolescence, sibling relationships, together with some especially close friendships, may form an 'inner circle' where compassion can be legitimately shown.

Oliver's narrative about the afternoons he spends with his little sister before their parents return from work is rare in that few of the participants assumed relatively regular caring responsibilities. His narrative differs from those of many of the other participants in that he seemed to willingly take up the responsibilities of a big brother, in contrast to the narrative of 'preferring being with friends to being with family' that many participants espoused. This further illustrates siblingships as one sphere with potential – although often unrealised – for more 'caring masculinities' (Elliott, 2016).

Oliver: [Sister] also comes [home from the school's afternoon club] usually when I'm already at home, she's [there] until my school day is over.

MP: Yes, okay so that she comes when you're there too, is it a bit like that you're taking care of her as the big brother?

Oliver: Yes.

MP: Do you have some common things with your sister that you do or are you then just, doing some things of your own?

Oliver: Well sometimes own things and then sometimes we do things together. I mean for example, if I play some video game then she watches when I play and cheers, and then I let her try to play as well. (…)

MP: Well what would you say, are you usually more at home like just with the family or your sister or with your friends or is it like both. How does it go?

Oliver: Well during the week, well yes I'm then probably more at home but in the weekends then I'm quite a lot [out], when my parents are at home as well so I can go everywhere, with my friends.

MP: Do you have some rules that, you can't go before telling your parents?

Oliver: Well I can go but then when my little sister comes home she doesn't want to be alone so I must stay with her.

MP: Yes, well I do understand, yes. Is it just an okay thing in your opinion, does it ever irritate?

Oliver: No it doesn't really irritate me. (*Individual interview Oliver, 12 years, mixed parentage, Harju School*)

Gaming – an activity that throughout the study was considered masculine – is another example of an activity that clearly had a gendered role in sibling relationships. Boys considered gaming to be masculine territory that girls (whether sisters or friends, see Chapter 5) could follow and sometimes try out, as in the case of Oliver above. However, in the few interviews with girls it was evident that some girls also enjoyed gaming – often with their brothers:

Elsa: I have a ten-year-old little brother and I don't know, we are like really close. We do everything stupid in secret and, agree, like if my brother has for example, a gaming ban then if he gives me candy, so I let him play. (…) With my brother I can always play all kinds of games and, like [it's] a lot more fun. (*Focus group 4, 2 boys 2 girls, 12–13 years, Finnish background, Nurmi School*)

In a focus group discussion with a 15-year-old trans boy and a girl, gaming was brought up as an activity in which both their little brothers had 'always' been engaged:

Sami: My little brother has always been the player. I was a bit interested in it myself too, I have been playing since I was small a lot of games at my friend's and at home, but my mum didn't really realize it at first. So she bought my little brother the games that he loved, which I was not interested in at all so I didn't get to play. Then my little brother owned the PlayStation and so on that I never got to play. (…)

Katriina: I was not really interested in [gaming] when I was smaller, but then when I got interested in it so it was a bit like that, my little brother just will always be a better player than I am because he has been playing since he was two and I started at 14. And then it's a bit like that, I don't want my little brother to be really better than me in something, and then it's just that you have to prove yourself especially when I'm a girl so I have to be good so that I have to show that girl can also be good. But when [laughs] I'm not, so then it is… (*Focus group 7, a girl and a trans boy, 15 years, Finnish background, Keinu youth club*)

In both the extracts above, it seemed that the younger boys' interests in gaming had always been self-evident to the parents, whereas the interviewees themselves had only later managed to establish more opportunities to play games and gain access to more interesting games to play. Katriina felt some resentment that she was apparently not constructed as fitting into the category of a gamer because she was a girl, especially since this meant being viewed as inferior to her little brother in this regard. Gaming is, thus, one of the sites where parents and young people negotiate and (re)produce or challenge gendered power relations.

Age was another important factor that shaped sibling relationships and roles. As might be predicted, sibling relationships were considerably different when the participants had older siblings. For Elias, for instance, his big brother was a figure who had superior knowledge about coolness, and someone who would potentially get embarrassed if Elias was seen in the wrong kind of clothes:

Elias: I don't know anything about clothes. [laughs] My big brother knows everything, so I ask him about everything. (…)

MP: Okay you said that you don't know much about clothes but is it that you ask your brother about which are— [fashionable]?

Elias: My brother knows everything so he tells me. And even if I don't ask him he'd still tell me. Sometimes, like he doesn't want me to wear some weird clothes cause people probably know that I am his brother. (*Individual interview Elias, 13 years, Finnish background, Nurmi School*)

While Elias deferred to his older brother's superior knowledge about fashion, his brother clearly constituted a social resource as suggested by Gillies and Lucey (2006). In contrast, Martin considered his older sister simply 'bossy' and prone to ordering him about. Martin was a rare exception in the sample in that in his description of his relationship with his older sister there were almost no positive feelings and he did not consider his sister to have any positive feelings about him:

Martin: Yea. She is very bossy.

MP: Bossy? She orders you around?

Martin: Yea but then I completely ignore her.

MP: You think it is because she is a girl or is it just, that she happens to be that way?

Martin: She is as she is on the inside. As she surely hates me someplace inside her. (*Individual interview Martin, 15 years, Estonian background, Kukkula School*)

Some of the participants had siblings who were considerably older than them. For instance, Mikko had, for a short time, shared an apartment with his older brother, who at the time of the interviews lived independently in another city. When asked if he had other close adults in his life, besides his parents and step-parents, Mikko said that since he had not lived 'brother life' with his brother he considered his brother not as a brother but a close adult. This did not mean, however, that considerably older siblings were not significant in the boys' lives. Aleksi, whose older brother also lived in another city, took care to visit him every day when he stayed with his parents at their cottage near to where his brother lives. He also acknowledged that his brother influenced both minor and major choices he has made, or plans to make:

> Aleksi: I do have like, a couple of basketball players they are, in a way, idols. Kobe Bryant comes to mind first at least.
>
> MP: Is it because he can play so well or?
>
> Aleksi: Yeah and he's also my brother's favourite player and then I remember when I was really small, and my brothers were about my age, so we were bought like a poster of Kobe Bryant and some team jerseys so, from that it kind of came like that I started to seek information about him. Then as soon as I started basketball then, I was in a way immediately excited about it. (…) When I was younger I wanted to be a doctor. Now it's a bit more, I would want to be a physiotherapist. Or physical education instructor or some teacher, because my brother is studying at the moment in [vocational school] to be a PE teacher or instructor I don't know what it is. But that could be quite fun as well. (*Individual interview Aleksi, 12 years, Finnish background, Nurmi School*)

While sibling relationships are generally under-researched in social research, masculinities and femininities are intertwined with gendered practices in sibling as well as other social relationships (Edwards et al., 2005). The boys were, however, as consistent in what they said about siblings in gendered terms as they were about their other social relationships in the rest of the interviews. Constructions of themselves as masculine and distancing themselves from femininity were a consistent feature of their narratives of sibling relationships.

## In Conclusion

In this chapter we have used the participants' narratives to step outside the confines of school and the normative restrictions of hegemonic masculinities. In doing so, we gain insights into how the participants see themselves and their social relations when they are not among peers who are highly sensitive to gendered expectations. In their homes they do not have to be careful to avoid breaching these expectations for fear of being derided and losing their positioning in the masculine hierarchies (re)produced in their schools and classes.

Drawing attention to boys' relationships with parents and siblings at home highlights three sets of issues germane to the relational 'doing' of masculinities. First, it illuminates how masculinities are intersectional in how space (home compared with school) and temporality (the age and sibling positioning of the participants) intersect with gendered relations. In keeping with other studies that have explored boys' relations with their parents, we found that the performativity of masculinity was different in relation to mothers and to fathers (Frosh et al., 2002). Participants' relationships with mothers were more domestic and focused on the household. They were more likely to consider that they could confide in their mothers than their fathers (even if they did not) and they explored an active, sporting world with their fathers, which they considered fun. This paralleled the gender differentiation they negotiated and reproduced at school.

The exploration of home narratives helped us to identify a second way in which boys 'did' masculinities in relation to their families. It was clear that boys saw themselves on a life course trajectory in which they were beginning to privilege their everyday relationships with their peers over those with their parents. One reason for this was that they could not risk telling their parents much about their lives in case they implicated other boys. Since most did not have confiding relations with other boys, this removed an important avenue for emotional engagement and understanding. Boys were mostly clear that they could tell their parents and gain support if something was wrong, but the everyday practices of emotionality were increasingly closed to them as they practised masculinities. Third, we also noticed an absence: joking, so central to the negotiation of masculinities at school, was not such an issue at home, even though fathers (and sometimes brothers) were often considered fun. It seems likely that one reason for this is that masculine hierarchies are not at issue in the same way at home and are not at the heart of acceptance and positioning at home, where age, gender and positioning in the sibling generation were more settled.

Overall, our engagement with boys' narratives of home and families helped to illuminate a complex, dynamic picture of how masculinities are negotiated and of how boys learn to nuance their masculinities and understand gendered relations over time by having access to different sites. It highlighted the importance of considering masculinities as negotiated in different places and multiple social relations as well as changing over time.

CHAPTER 8

# Narratives of Multiculturalism

The 2020 Black Lives Matter protests following the murder of George Floyd by the white policeman Derek Chauvin in Minneapolis, Minnesota, produced an unprecedented and global appetite to understand the specificities and ubiquity of racism in its subtle, mundane materialisations as well as its murderous manifestations. The resulting outpouring of testimonies from black and mixed-parentage people as well as from people in other minoritised ethnic groups has shifted understandings of historical social relations and of the complexity and plurality of racisms. One perhaps unexpected outcome has been recognition that the invisibility of racism to some of those who are never subjected to it and the lack of social acknowledgement of it does not mean either that it does not exist, or that it does not continue to have marked impacts on society and social relations. As Avery Gordon suggests, these forms of subjugated knowledge haunt society:

> The first [aspect] is that the ghost is not, as I see it, the invisible or the unknown or the absent per se. Ghosts appear when the trouble they represent and symptomize is no longer contained or repressed or blocked from view. In other words, haunting is a way we're notified that what's been suppressed or concealed is very much alive and present, interfering with us and with the systems of repression that produce concealment and blockage. The second aspect is (...) a sociopolitical–psychological state

> when something else or something different from before feels like it must be done and prompts a something-to-be-done. (Gordon, Hite and Jara, 2020: 339)

Gordon's notion may seem more relevant in countries with long and undeniable histories of colonialism and racism. However, it alerts us to the salience of racialisation and racisms, even when unacknowledged. For the young people in our study, this period of growing up in a culture newly recognising itself as multicultural is, therefore, important for what it will mean for Finnish futures and what will haunt society in generations to come.

The participants in this study are living their youth at a time when the percentage of people from minoritised ethnic groups, including visibly minoritised groups, is increasing, particularly in urban areas like Helsinki and especially among younger age groups (see Chapter 1). For that reason, some young people are beginning to think about, and learning to live, multicultures and multiculturalism. However, even in Helsinki, many white Finnish young people have little experience of people from other ethnic groups.

In Finland, the myth of 'monoculture' has been cherished since the nationalist movements of the 19th century (Tervonen, 2014), and in the public imaginary it has largely overshadowed Finland's multicultural history with the indigenous Sami and minorities of Roma, Tatars, Russians and Jews (e.g. Martikainen, Sintonen and Pitkänen, 2006). Finland remained characterised by emigration rather than immigration until the turn of the 1980s and 1990s, and the low percentage of the population 'with foreign backgrounds' has, at least partly, helped to maintain the myth of Finland as an ethnically homogeneous country. Since the beginning of the 1990s, a steady increase in immigration has served to intensify discussions concerning ethnic and cultural diversity in Finland. In addition, discussions on racism and anti-racism have largely been absent, until recently (e.g. Keskinen, 2018).

As part of the reimagining of the 'new', more multicultural Finland, the younger generations are often accorded special status. One popular narrative assumes that Finnish children and young people (who are still implicitly assumed to be white) are 'doing' multiculturalism in ways their parents' generation are not. In other words, unlike older generations, they attend multicultural educational institutions and other contexts and are, therefore, assumed to be growing up 'tolerant' and living multi-ethnicity as 'normal'. As a consequence, they are considered a generation who will disrupt racialised divides and make racism obsolete. In that context, some teachers are resistant to acknowledge ethnicised and racialised differences between children and praise those who profess colour blindness (Kimanen, 2018).

This chapter examines the participants' narratives of multiculturalism. It argues that they are intersectional, dependent on generation, temporality, social class, space (e.g. school, hobbies and restaurants), gender and the specificity of place (Helsinki), as well as ethnicity.

## Multi-ethnicity in Schools

The three schools where most of the interviews were carried out differed from each other in terms of the ethnic mix of the pupils, among other things. This meant that the interviewees in the three schools differed in how likely it was that they could encounter and interact with young people from ethnic groups other than their own. This was, to a certain extent, reflected in their narratives about multiculturalism in their schools.

For those young people, boys and girls, living and going to Nurmi School in a wealthy (upper-)middle-class white area, multi-ethnicity was not part of their everyday lives. In a focus group with four ethnically Finnish young people, two boys and two girls, a question on 'multiculturalism' (*monikulttuurisuus*, the term most commonly used in Finland) raised the following discussion:

MP: What about then, multiculturalism, is that a thing that is visible in this school in any way?

Sofia: What do you mean?

MP: Like, that, are there any pupils with different backgrounds and different ethn—?

Elsa/Veeti [simultaneously] Well quite a little…

Sofia: Do you mean like religion?

MP: Well religion or then, if you think like, if there's people who have moved here from somewhere else or their parents have moved here or like that.

Veeti: Well I don't really know anyone's origins. I know only that, two people have different religions [classes] and then, I… That's it.

Sofia: Well I know, I've seen on the school hallways for example a couple, only some three or four people who use a kind of veil. But no one probably goes to say to them anything, hopefully or like that. So it's like that everybody adjusts to this [school]. (*Focus group 4, 2 boys 2 girls, 12–13 years, Finnish background, Nurmi School*)

After some uncertainty, the interviewees came up with examples of individual pupils (or teachers) who represented 'multiculturalism' to them. Multiculturalism was not considered relevant for the school as a whole or something the young people considered relevant to them. It was, instead, seen as exceptional and as embodied in the very few individuals in the school who, either by wearing a hijab or by attending religious classes other than Evangelical Lutheran, were viewed as 'different'. In other words, they considered that certain people personified difference from what they considered the Finnish norm. The norm of white Finnishness was strong and unquestioned. Sofia, for instance, while hoping that 'no one goes to say anything [negative] to them', takes it for granted that it is those who are seen as different from the norm who should 'adjust'.

Among the interviewees in Nurmi School, understanding multiethnicity as something removed from everyday life was related both to the composition of the school and the area more generally. For some, out-of-school hobbies offered possibilities to meet young people from different backgrounds. In the extract below, however, Aleksi explained that, even in that case, it was not necessarily easy to form closer friendships, since boys from minoritised ethnic groups and backgrounds other than Finnish typically lived further away from the school and the hobbies he did than the white Finnish boys did and so they were not part of everyday life outside school and the hobby:

> Aleksi: Yeah in the basketball team there are at least five [players with backgrounds other than Finnish]. No we have more, a couple of Russians a couple of Frenchmen and then two from America.
>
> MP: Are you ever in touch with them other than in basketball?
>
> Aleksi: I am. [But] it's like a bit of a problem with those basketball friends because some come from so far, like from [area in Helsinki]. So in comparison [to others], you rarely see them in your free time. (*Individual interview Aleksi, 12 years, Finnish background, Nurmi School*)

For others, the pervasiveness of the white Finnish norm extended to the sphere of the hobby. For instance, Veeti, in his individual interview, was particularly reflexive about white middle-class participants' relationship with multiculturalism. In the extract below he explained that it was very difficult for him to get to know 'dark-skinned' people since he never saw them anywhere:

> Veeti: Well actually I don't have dark-skinned friends at all. I have even never, I don't, I wouldn't have any chance to get any dark-skinned friends. (...) I don't have any in my immediate circles, so I have never seen here in the nearby areas in any hobby any, for example a dark-skinned person. In jujitsu there are a couple of people, but they only speak English and they are mainly just in their own circles. Here in school I don't have [any], in any of the seventh grade classes you can't see any dark-skinned people, at least as far as I have seen. Then I don't have any in football, so it's really hard for me to get to know that kind of person. (*Individual interview Veeti, 13 years, Finnish background, Nurmi School*)

Veeti's narrative in the extract above distances 'dark-skinned' people from himself because they are mostly geographically separate. His views on multiculturalism should not, however, be read only as resulting from his living in a white area. He made it clear that social class intersected with racialisation and gender in conditioning his experiences and views. His position as an upper-middle-class boy was clearly part of his identities and he explained that his family were very well travelled, so that he had experience of different cultures, especially food, outside Finland. Veeti understood multiculturalism not only in relation to the migration of people but also in terms of migration of commodities and ideas. He welcomed, for instance, the increased presence of more diverse food cultures in Finland (commodities he could consume), yet was more suspicious of diversifying religious life and using 'public money' to fund the building of a mosque, something he did not see as necessary on the scale intended:

MP: Is multiculturalism in general the kind of thing that's like familiar to you or have you ever thought about it?

Veeti: It is familiar because we travel so much, so of course I then eat ... there some more multicultural food and especially because my parents don't like these tourist places at all, for example some touristy restaurant, or well that's probably the biggest thing that my parents don't like about touristy places. And then tourist beaches are annoying according to them, they like more like, for example if we go to some country so we eat quite a lot of the country's food. For example, in Japan, we ate quite a lot of Japanese food, like for example the kind of a sushi conveyor. We didn't eat in any of the kind of European type of sushi places, so we had like we tried to eat food as Japanese as possible, because that is usually then the best. (...)

MP: Do you have any opinion about the fact that Finland is now becoming multicultural. Is it a good or a bad thing?

Veeti: Well I think it's quite a good thing. I'm quite excited that for example that Taco Bell is coming. Do you know the American chain? So that's coming to Finland now and, I like it that at least in food culture that Finland is becoming multicultural and then it's quite interesting as well, it's not a bad thing at all I think. But then if you start to use a lot of money, or like really a lot of money for religions, for example I was a bit pensive about what was it again the chapel.

MP: The mosque project?

Veeti: Yeah about that. I was a bit like quite a lot of money will probably be spent on that. It isn't in the end probably that much, but it was immediately the first thought that is that now so wise? Because there aren't that many probably here in the end. So you could maybe make it a bit smaller. But yeah.

From time to time, it is argued in Finland (as elsewhere) that young people are already living multicultural lives, and therefore they will grow up to be a 'tolerant' generation that is better equipped to promote ethnic equality in Finnish society. Just as the assumption that the young generation are necessarily open-minded and mix easily is too simplistic (Janmaat and Keating, 2019), the assumption that most young people are already familiar with multi-ethnicity also seems somewhat misplaced. Veeti's narrative (above) reproduces the notion that whiteness is the norm and minoritised ethnic groups are outsiders to the Finnish state. As the extract shows, even in the metropolitan area of Helsinki, which is one of the most ethnically diverse areas of Finland, there are white Finnish areas where young people have little (if any) contact with people from other ethnicities than Finnish in their immediate, everyday life. This, once again, highlights differences between young people.

While multi-ethnicity was clearly a distant theme for those white Finnish young people who lived and went to school in the white, upper-middle-class area, it is noteworthy that, even in the two other, more ethnically mixed schools, the participants generally did not have the vocabulary to think about, and analyse, multi-ethnicity in their schools or in the society. For most white Finnish young people we interviewed, the norm of whiteness went unnoticed and unquestioned, and multi-ethnicity was a theme that did not really concern them, even in school contexts where different ethnicities were more visibly present. Research in schools has shown that multi-ethnicity/multiculturalism, racism and anti-racism figure very little in Finnish school curricula (Alemanji, 2016; Souto, 2011). Young people who are interested in these topics may use the internet or other sources to increase their understanding. For others, we found that multi-ethnicity remains a shallow and distant issue that they struggled to talk about unless concepts, narratives, examples, and vocabulary were offered by the interviewer.

Despite this general absence of multi-ethnic consciousness, place did make a difference to the boys' narratives. The white Finnish boys in the more multi-ethnic schools reflected somewhat more on multicultures in their school. In the following focus group discussion in a school in a more mixed area, the two Finnish boys, Onni and Lauri, presented representations of 'immigrant' boys:

MP: Is this school in your opinion so-called multicultural, whatever that means to you?

Lauri: Yes. [others agree]

MP: How does that show here?

Lauri: Well everybody gets along but it may be that some people, particular people, maybe if… (…) those who have come from somewhere abroad so they try to take a role, at least some.

Onni: Yeah, really a lot.

MP: What sort of roles?

Onni: Well like they start to throw their weight about, terribly much. Probably just so they are not as targets of such behaviour, but in my opinion there's almost none of that at all here in my school. I don't say now that everybody's doing that but quite often when that comes from somewhere, generally it is from the immigrants. …

MP: If you think about the teachers, does it show in any way in their behaviour that people come from different backgrounds? Is it so-called equal here, the treatment?

Lauri: It depends a bit, it may be a bit stricter for the foreigners. But it may well depend on their own behaviour. (*Focus group 5, 5 boys, 14–15 years, 4 with Finnish backgrounds, one with migrant parents, Kukkula School)*

In the above focus group, Lauri and Onni agreed that their school is multicultural and, when asked how that is evident, Lauri explained that they all get along, but immediately made exceptions by explaining that 'particular people (…) come from somewhere abroad so they try to take a role'. It is noteworthy that, while he quickly explains what multicultural means, his engagement with difference is less fluent in that he stops, restarts, talks about 'some people', 'particular people', then 'at least some' when making a distinction between some of those who come from abroad and, implicitly, presumably white Finnish people. Unlike the clarity of his statement that multicultural means that everybody gets along, the rest of his first response is far from clear to the interviewer or reader, although it seemed clear to Onni in the group, who said, 'Yeah, really a lot'. When the interviewer asked for clarification, it was Onni who responded with a long turn explaining that 'they start to throw their weight around, terribly much'. Just as Lauri seemed to have felt impelled to give an explanatory extension to his first statement, so Onni provided an explanation of his first answer that the people he is talking about might 'throw their weight around'. His explanation suggests that this may be because 'they' are targets for other people. However, having implicitly suggested that boys identified as 'immigrants' may be badly treated by white Finnish people, he explains that this does not happen in his school and that, while not all 'immigrants' are like this, any problems are caused by 'the immigrants'. When the interviewer follows this up by asking whether teachers treat everyone equally, Lauri explains that 'it may be a bit stricter for the foreigners' but that this is probably contingent on 'their own behaviour'.

The effect of this exchange is to maintain white Finnishness as the norm and 'immigrants' and 'foreigners' as problematic by comparison without having a good reason for being so. In these exchanges, both Lauri and Onni smoothed over contradictions by recognising that 'other' young people may be treated badly while either denying that it happens in their school or suggesting that it only occurs as a response to those young people's unacceptable behaviour.

While exchanges such as those above were common in the study, in the same focus group discussion, Martin, who has Estonian-Russian parentage, diversified the understanding of multiculture in the school. He made suppositions about different possible backgrounds for the other (white Finnish) boys in the focus group and pointed out that, besides differences in ethnic background, there may also be differences in areas of origin or occupational and family backgrounds:

> Martin: For example we could be versatile because maybe Joel comes [from a family of] a farmer who lives in the forest and then Eino's dad is a bear hunter and then, we are from different backgrounds, but our, we are still multicultural because we are of different things and we have different customs. (*Focus group 5, 5 boys, 14–15 years, 4 with Finnish backgrounds, one with migrant parents, Kukkula School*)

Martin's point that 'we are still multicultural' serves to resist the othering of migrants and, psychosocially, to include himself as ordinary among his peers. In Butler's (2004) terms, he claimed recognition for himself in the story of the culture and inclusion in liveable life.

## Egalitarian Multicultural Ideology

Just as the boys produced narratives of commitment to gender equality when asked in general (Chapter 3), so too were they committed to an egalitarian multicultural ideology. The most frequent narratives can be characterised as an 'all different, all equal' type of argumentation in which they suggested that ethnic background does not matter in friendships or social relationships at large.

For instance, 14-year-old Lauri – who in general gave only brief reflections – spoke about multi-ethnicity in his school in a rather matter-of-fact way, as a phenomenon that does not really influence either social relations in the school or how pupils are treated there. Yet, further probing nuanced his answer somewhat.

MP: Yes, what about how if you think about your friends are there so-called not Finnish or some people who would have moved here from elsewhere?

Lauri: Yes there are some.

MP: At this school there are probably still like quite a lot.

Lauri: Yes.

MP: What do you think, is it a good thing for the school's atmosphere?

Lauri: Yes it's a pretty good thing.

MP: Do you think that… Are people different according to what their background is?

Lauri: They usually blend in, the people in a way with the group.

MP: So that doesn't matter?

Lauri: Yes.

MP: Do you think that here at school, are they treated just the same way or equally so-called?

Lauri: Well in my opinion quite equally, like the same way.

MP: Yes. And you wouldn't see either that they would have some specific, if you think people who have moved here, that they would represent some specific style or do they have some things of their own or?

Lauri: Well yes they have sometimes some of their own things or then they like to stay only with others who have foreign backgrounds.

MP: Is it that these are their friends, or are they a bit like different anyway?

Lauri: Yes in my opinion.

MP: Why do you think that is?

Lauri: I don't really know.

MP: Yes. But, if you think of your friends, does it to like matter to you what their ethnicity is?

Lauri: It doesn't matter in my opinion. (*Individual interview Lauri, 14 years, Finnish background, Kukkula School*)

Lauri started his narrative by refuting notions that either people with 'foreign backgrounds' are different or are treated differently in the school. However, when asked whether people who had moved to Finland from elsewhere had any 'things of their own', Lauri said that they liked to be with other foreign people, contradicting what he had just said about 'blending in'. It is noteworthy that, as when the boys talked about 'self-segregating girls' (see Chapter 3), in Lauri's narrative it is the 'foreign' pupils who he said liked to be with others with foreign backgrounds. He did not mention the possibility that Finnish pupils might do anything to cause this outsider grouping by having similar preferences themselves or by being exclusionary. When asked, he explained that this informal segregation does not matter.

Liban, who was Finnish with Somali parents, reflected further on the positive aspects of a multi-ethnic school context that Lauri had mentioned but not elaborated on. He suggested that it helped to meet people with different opinions and so to see things from different perspectives. As suggested by Aaltonen et al. (2011), there seems to be an emphasis on individual qualities, like sociability, in how social relations are explained as working in the multi-ethnic school. The benefits of knowing different people and different perspectives arise from being able to 'talk and get to know' people. Liban, who was black, was adamant that skin colour did not matter at school:

MP: How, would you say that this, your school is so called multicultural or are there lots of people from different backgrounds here or?

Liban: Yes I feel that there are lots of different people. As long as you just manage to talk and get to know them.

MP: Does it affect the school's atmosphere in any way?

Liban: I don't think that it affects. (...) Yes, it does in a good way but I don't think that in any bad one. (...)

MP: What do you see yourself that, what good can it bring to the school?

Liban: Well, for example if everyone had the same background, then they would probably have the same opinions on things, you know, but when everyone has different backgrounds, all have different opinions and then in some things it helps to see, from different perspectives, which is probably a good thing, [laughs] or I mean it is a good thing.

MP: Yes it is, it widens the kind of, perspective, right. Do you have friends like, what would you say, are they from different backgrounds or are they from the same background as you for example?

Liban: No. I have, I have quite, many kind of friends.

MP: Yes, are they mostly Finnish?

Liban: No, I do have Finnish, from everywhere probably, well not really everywhere but I do like, really different.

MP: Does skin colour or that kind of thing matter at this point?

Liban: No. No, it doesn't matter. (*Individual interview Liban, 14 years, Somali background, Kukkula School*)

Unlike Lauri, in his individual interview, Liban emphasised the school's multi-ethnic composition and presents a narrative of it as undoubtedly beneficial. His statement 'Yes I feel that there are lots of different people. As long as you just manage to talk and get to know them' is somewhat enigmatic since there are a variety of people at his school, even if other people do not manage to talk with them or get to know them. It would appear that he was proleptically defending against the possibility that the interviewer would problematise multiculturalism by blaming people with 'different backgrounds' for being separatist. Like the white Finnish boys, Liban maintained that skin colour does not matter, but, since his narrative of multiculturalism differed from those of the white Finnish boys in the study, he performatively showed that positioning, and so colour, does matter. This is further exemplified in the next extract, where two white Finnish boys espoused multicultural equality.

In the white, (upper-)middle-class Nurmi School, Valtteri and Kristian, too, sought to represent themselves as accepting of differences and argue that it is individual qualities – what is inside one's head – that matters, not ethnicised/racialised/migratory background. Valtteri also criticised Finnish people for complaining about immigrants, which he thought was stupid. Despite Valtteri's manifest opposition to racist discrimination, the presence of non-Finnish people in Finland seemed acceptable only because of their small number and because they did not cause 'harm'. Their acceptance is, therefore, conditional.

> MP: How about here in school, can you see multiculturalism…?
>
> Kristian: It isn't necessarily that multicultural here.
>
> Valtteri: Here there is quite a lot of, the same Finnish people, like all, I see a lot of those comments [on the internet] where people complain that how many, immigrants there supposedly are here and everything really horrible, so I think, here after all there aren't a lot and I think they're not causing any harm even. And, like there aren't that many here either so, really there aren't a lot…
>
> Kristian: It depends on what is there inside, inside the head.
>
> Valtteri: Yeah, I think so too, it doesn't matter at all, that, like I don't get how it could matter at all, to some. (*Focus group 4, 2 boys, 12 years, Finnish background, Nurmi School*)

Many of the white Finnish participants took a colour-blind approach at the level of an 'all different, all equal' rhetoric because their whiteness enabled them to take for granted their Finnishness and belonging in Finnish society. Colour-blind approaches have been widely critiqued as a form of racism that obscures, while perpetuating, the normative positioning of whiteness and the existence of racialised inequalities and racism (e.g. Bonilla-Silva and Dietrich, 2011). These accounts therefore implicitly reproduce the racialised status quo and, as found in much work on whiteness, makes their undoubted commitment to egalitarian ideologies and eschewing of racism contingent and limited (Leonardo, 2009; Nayak, 2007).

In some cases, egalitarian multicultural ideologies also gave the white interviewees tools for resisting racist stereotyping. Johannes's criticism of stereotyping 'Africans' as terrorists (below) presents a particularly clear case of this antiracist narrative built around the notion that people are good or bad individuals regardless of their origins:

> Johannes: Also Finns can basically just as well be something that immigrants can be… the same way. Probably about the immigrants so yes there are good people but then there are also those bad people too but the same is in Finland as well, that here is also like that. Basically it's a small stereotype that a terrorist is, some African. It isn't [so] basically. Yeah, like a Finn can just as well be a terrorist when, there have been [the cases in which Finnish people have] thrown everything at those immigrant offices [meaning asylum-seekers' reception centres]. It's just the same kind of terrorism. (*Individual interview Johannes, 13 years, Finnish background, Nurmi School*)

## Eschewing Racism

The egalitarian multicultural ideology that the participants embraced was connected to their eschewing of racism. While racism was seen vaguely as 'bad' and to be avoided, it was also largely understood as an individual phenomenon (rather than a structural one) that was nothing to do with the participants themselves.

The following extract is from a focus group discussion in the school located in the white, upper-middle-class area. The group of four boys had just agreed together that ethnic background 'doesn't matter', immediately after which Elmeri gave an example of racist behaviour that had taken place within his football hobby. While Elmeri described the behaviour as 'a bit racist' and 'dumb', he told the story in a trivialising way – not pointing out any need for condemnation, taking a stand, or intervening:

> MP: Have you ever encountered something that people whose origins are somewhere else were treated in a different way than…?
>
> Elmeri: Yeah.
>
> MP: Okay, where?
>
> Elmeri: Well we have one like a dark-skinned forward. He's really good at running so people always shout at him everything like, go steal bikes and then, everything else a bit racist like this.
>
> MP: Ok so some opponents shout or?
>
> Elmeri: Opponents and then some parents shout.
>
> MP: Parents, for real?
>
> Elmeri: Yeah and sometimes in school people throw bananas at him and [laughs] other stuff like this.
>
> MP: Right. Has your, coach or someone said something about it?
>
> Elmeri: Yes but it doesn't help at all when, they just don't listen.
>
> MP: Well what do you think about it?
>
> Elmeri: I think it's a bit dumb but, not everyone needs to be friends with everyone. (*Focus group 3, 4 boys, 13 years, three with Finnish background, one mixed parentage, Nurmi School*)

In this narrative, Elmeri did not himself take any active position apart from as an observer. He did not express any sense that he should show opposition to such behaviour either during the event or when recounting it in the interview situation. Neither did he expect real opposition or intervention from the coach, whom he agreed did say 'something', but whom he rendered powerless by pointing out that the coach could not help that since the people making the racist comments 'don't listen'. When asked to reflect on the issue himself, Elmeri framed it again as an individual-level problem relating to the nature of people's relationships. He said nothing about the power dynamics involved in adults subjecting a child to racism and referred to racism as if it only occurs when people are not 'friends', while making it clear that he considered it unreasonable to expect that everyone should be friends.

Elmeri himself remained removed from the whole issue, 'an innocent bystander'. The role of an innocent bystander also meant that the boys did not feel they had either the responsibility or possibility of protesting against incidents that most people would recognise as racist.

> MP: What do you think about that, does your background matter anything here at school?
>
> Daniel: Well, no.
>
> MP: Like you are considered just like, like everyone else?
>
> Daniel: M-mm [agreeing]. But if those who are for example dark-skinned or something, may sometimes have that n-word shouted at you. (…)
>
> MP: There is quite a lot talk in the media, like for example about racism and this and that and so, have you ever thought about it, generally?
>
> Daniel: You mean racism?
>
> MP: Yes.
>
> Daniel: Well I haven't… I mean, everyone is equal but I haven't more, like, I mean I don't start going to streets and shout that racism is wrong, so. (*Individual interview Daniel, 13 years, mixed parentage, Nurmi School*)

Daniel, who was of Asian-Finnish parentage and among the very few pupils with minoritised ethnic backgrounds in his school, might also have distanced himself from antiracist action because he did not wish to draw additional attention to the ways in which he deviated from the pervasive white Finnish norm in his school (see Rastas, 2007). These interviews were conducted before the resurgence of Black Lives Matter protests following the 2020 murder of George Floyd by a policeman in the US. We do not, therefore, know what Daniel would now say about those who are 'dark-skinned' being called the 'N' word or whether he would now protest or feel that it is unacceptable, even if he did not challenge it.

White Finnish boys in the study sometimes denied that particular behaviours that some people might consider racist were so. This happened often in the context of talking about 'joking' in which they were involved. According to the boys, using racist language in a joking way was much like using any other insult: it was not serious or 'really racist' since everybody knew it was joking. For instance, Onni – who strongly embraced egalitarian ideals, in relation to both gender and multicultures – knew that the language they used with his team members could be interpreted as racist, yet denied racism, because the words, according to him, could not be taken seriously since they were such good friends.

> MP: Have you ever heard that any of them would face some racism or something, shouting for example in some your matches?
>
> Onni: No, I haven't and then just, in the workouts it doesn't, if someone says something so called that could be in someone's opinion so it's still, we're all such good friends with each other that it, it just doesn't influence in any way that, or if, everyone there, so if you say something about another so it's always joking, like in our team, there it's not worth it to take anything seriously, it's a bit like that. (*Individual interview Onni, 13 years, Finnish background, Kukkula School*)

Thirteen-year-old Samu positioned himself in a very similar manner, describing how in the football team 'everyone is dissed equally' and therefore this is nothing to get offended about. He also makes a distinction between young people and the adult generation and explains that 'real' or 'severe' racism is more common among adults. In a similar way, several interviewees were of the opinion that racism is something that is mostly visible on the internet. While the argument that adults are more racist than young people follows the common narrative of 'children living in multicultural environments and thus growing up to be more "tolerant"', it is also one way of locating racism outside of one's own sphere, as a phenomenon that does not have relevance for oneself (Alemanji and Dervin, 2016):

> MP: Right. Well have you ever then seen like that someone, for example those friends of yours who have parents from somewhere else, that they would've been dissed, called names or something?
>
> Samu: Noo, not really in any particular way, so it isn't. In the team as well there are of course [people] from some other countries as well but, no, people don't make any racist jokes about them, and of course at times it can be like, but that's more the kind of within the group of friends like internal that everyone is dissed equally, and like that as a joke, but you have learned to know your friends so well that then like, they don't in a way get offended by it, so it's like… (…) More it is like that if something is really like dissing or racist then it comes more from adults or like that, but it's not, of course, children have it at times too, but it's not at all as like in any way as strong, or at least with my friends. So it's not in any way like that. (*Individual interview Samu, 13 years, Finnish background, Nurmi School*)

In this context, Samu took pains to interpret name-calling that could be considered racist as part of the broader narrative of joking that was central to masculine performativity (see Chapter 3). Masculine norms demand that the jokes are 'got' – otherwise joking does not fulfil its purpose in masculine performance and boys who fail to take jokes are also viewed as failing at being properly masculine. For the minoritised ethnic boys who were visibly identifiable by the white Finnish boys, this meant that 'joking' that included racist language added a layer to what they had to endure as an everyday part of masculinity-building practices. Fourteen-year-old Yonas (below) had, earlier in the interview, reflected on the negative consequences of masculine joking that is difficult to challenge:

> Yonas: Well not really so that there was racism or something like that, I haven't really heard that. But just joking I have heard.
>
> MP: What have you thought then, is it appropriate?
>
> Yonas: What?
>
> MP: When someone is joking about that?
>
> Yonas: Well I don't really when you think if it is ap— It's just joking so it doesn't mean that.
>
> MP: So it's just the same as the other irritating things?
>
> Yonas: Yes basically. (*Individual interview Yonas, 14 years, Eritrean background, Kukkula School*)

It may well be that, because Yonas was black, he agreed with the interviewer that racist joking is 'irritating', whereas his white peers resisted talking of it as anything other than 'joking'. However, in keeping with other boys' accounts, he denied that joking meant racism, although, since he stopped what he had been about to say, it is not entirely clear whether he had been about to say that it is not appropriate, but stopped himself, or whether he stopped in order to rephrase what he was saying as he thought about it. Discussion of racism with the white interviewer might, therefore, have put him into a troubled subject position (Wetherell, 2012).

The examples above show that the most common interpretations of ethnic inequalities and racism individualised them as individual problems or understood them as part of masculine joking that 'didn't matter'. Yet, Vilja, a 15-year-old girl in the sample, showed that white young people could be both analytic about racism and oppose it:

Vilja: I think it is also something like, about being a part of a group, I don't know. Like, sure it is fun for white boys to be racist and misogynist, like, yeah.

MP: What about the racism, how does that show itself?

Vilja: One guy from my class even compared dark-skinned people to animals, and sometimes, one of my good friends who is a Muslim, so, she has got a quite nasty set, and has to hear, too, for instance the n-word and that. But generally it is quite like, not that aggressive but like, casual racism. [laughs] Is that even a word? But like, that sort of general prejudice, or like, that discussion about refugees. (…) This same person who compared dark-skinned people to animals, then he was like 'that was a joke', like 'I have a black friend, too', so, like it was this eternal issue. (*Individual interview Vilja, 15 years, Finnish background*)

In the above example, while Vilja recognised and opposed racism, she distanced herself from racism. Thus, she discussed both blatant and more implicit racism in her predominantly white school as connected to masculine 'groupism' and (male) privilege and so nothing to do with girls.

This intersectional racialised and gendered perspective was also presented in a co-constructed focus group discussion with a boy (who had until recently been brought up as a girl) and his good (female) friend. They discussed racism in the school as related to the predominance of whiteness in some of the classes, to gender and to social class issues.

Sami: We have a ridiculously white school, or I mean Finland in general is very white. So then especially the sports class, they are all white. (…)

Katriina: Then also, they're also relatively wealthy, those in the sport class.

Sami: Yes they're all quite wealthy, they always have all the latest fashions, more new clothes and, good mobile phones and everything else like that. (…)

Katriina: Yes it's a bit, then also when they're– I don't know if they are racist or not, when they... well it seems to be a bit like that they are [racist], all of them, at least a bit.

MP: You mean who they?

Katriina: They...

Sami: Sport—

Katriina: Boys in the sports classes. And then also it feels, they are using it, for example we have one other, a ninth grader black boy, they have said the n-word [to him].

MP: Ah, oh no.

Sami: But I feel that, I don't know. [Boy name] for example wants so much acceptance that he er kind of like, accepts it. (...) And then at our school we have so many of those white sporty boys that all the non-white boys are gamer boys and then they're automatically a bit more feminine. Not necessarily more feminine but still feminine. (*Focus group 7, a trans boy and a girl, 15 years, Finnish background, Keinu youth club*)

According to Sami and Katriina, racist attitudes are common among white Finnish boys, particularly in the specialist sports class, where the boys are affluent and are considered to be at the top of the school hierarchy. Sami suggested that, despite the fact that some of the boys from minoritised ethnic groups were sometimes subjected to racist behaviour, they still sought to be accepted rather than complaining about the racism to which they were subject. According to Sami, the category of white sporting boys was so strong and masculine that, in comparison, all those he referred to as 'non-white' boys were lumped together as 'gamer boys', a category that is viewed in schools as less masculine. In Sami's and Katriina's narrative, racism was gendered as a masculine phenomenon and only discussed in relation to boys' behaviour and their social hierarchies.

Vilja and Sami and Katriina provided starkly different accounts from Samu's and Onni's. This may be because they came from different schools – they were interviewed at the youth club or at home and therefore their school was not one of the three schools that participated in the study. It may also be, however, because they had a different social understanding and had developed an intersectional racialised/social class analysis. This fits with Sami and Katriina's narrative that black boys are subjected to racism without having done anything to warrant it and that they do not retaliate but instead seek 'acceptance' from the powerful, white Finnish boys. It is also in line with their other accounts, as, quite exceptionally in the data, they adopted an intersectional view on many of the topics discussed and were sensitive to differences related to social class, ethnicity, skin colour, gender and sexuality and, as Vilja was, were opposed to all discriminatory practices. Their positioning as a girl and a boy who had had experience of living as a girl is likely to have had an impact on their narratives.

## In Conclusion

All the participants embraced egalitarian ideas of everybody being equal in some way. Yet, for many white Finns in particular, the concrete resources available to them (e.g. vocabularies, experiences with people from different backgrounds) for analysing issues related to ethnicities and multiculturalism were limited. In addition, the importance of joking for masculine performativity extended to the area of multiculturalism: the need to 'get' the joke remained crucial, even in cases where the joke could be considered racist. While the interviewees were not in favour of racism, calling it 'dumb', they did not actively oppose it. Rather, they positioned themselves as 'innocent outsiders' in relation to racism, taking an 'all different all equal' position. Yet, in the above examples, white Finnish boys constructed white Finnish masculinity as the norm, with other masculinities constructed in contrast as either excessive ('macho'/'troublemaker') or as feminine, something that is commonly found in research on masculinities in many countries.

# Endnote

We undoubtedly live in times more exciting than we might have wished. Two events that patterned the start of the third decade of the 2000s have relevance for the understanding of contemporary masculinities among boys. The coronavirus pandemic and the 2020 resurgence of Black Lives Matter following the killing of George Floyd by the Minnesota police in the USA both have resonances for the understanding of masculinities in the Finnish context, as elsewhere. Speaking of the differences that COVID-19 has illuminated, Raewyn Connell (2021: 2) pointed out that '[a]n emergency that seemed at first to have nothing to do with gender, thus turns out to have a lot to do with the situations of women and men'.

Equally, the racialised injustices illuminated in the Black Lives Matter movement also illuminate gender differences in that the killing of black men attracts much more attention than the killing of black women and children by US police – an inequality that led to the campaign #SayHerName, co-founded by Kimberlé Crenshaw, who coined the term intersectionality (Crenshaw, 2020).

These examples show the inextricable links between what happens to individuals and social processes, and the importance of intersectionality to the understanding of masculinities anywhere (Langa, 2020).

## Narrative Disruptions of Hegemonic, Toxic and Inclusive Essentialism

Masculinity has been the subject of much debate over the last 30 years. In many countries around the globe, boys and men have been the subject of concern about issues ranging from their relatively poorer educational attainment in relation to girls and women to their greater likelihood of perpetrating domestic and sexual violence and higher risks of suicide. Recognition of these links has often been constructed as a 'crisis of masculinity' and led to the popularisation of the term 'toxic masculinity' to indicate a combination of features associated with boys and men that include the suppressing of emotions, 'hardness' and exercising power through threats of violence (Salter, 2019). This combination of features has repeatedly been found in studies of men and boys and linked with the notion of 'hegemonic masculinity' that has run through the chapters above (Connell and Messerschmitt, 2005). 'Toxic masculinity' has repeatedly been associated with risk of mental health problems, violence and gender inequality in ways that have generated social concern in the media, among policymakers and in research. Indeed, the 'cool pose' that is associated with these features has also long been reported to prevent men from being aware of how they feel (Majors and Billson, 1993). It is this combination of factors that led the American Psychological Association (2018a) to produce ten guidelines for redressing toxic masculinity through psychological practice with boys and men with a view to improving boys' mental health and future prospects as well as gender relations and fatherhood. They have devised these guidelines based on their conclusion from the literature that:

> Understanding the connection between negative male socialization and violence calls us to support preventative strategies that:
>
> - Counter the problematic normative pressures boys face.
> - Recognize gender-related social norms and seek to change the way men view and express themselves resulting in a shift of gendered practices, including the use of violence. (American Psychological Association, 2018b)

'Toxic masculinity' is generally counterposed to notions of healthy masculinity in ways that essentialise masculinity and pay little regard to the insights produced by Connell's (1995) careful theorisation of masculinities as plural, rather than singular. Further, as was pointed out by de Boise (2019), the term 'toxic masculinity' tends to individualise and decontextualise the social problems it addresses. Connell (2020) showed that masculinities, like femininities, are relational, produced in everyday negotiations of practice in sociostructural contexts that vary by place and shift over time. While notions of 'hegemonic masculinities' can serve to define the standards and characteristics by which 'real men' are evaluated, boys and men often compete in claiming authentic masculinity. Hegemonic masculinities are also plural and, while features considered to characterise them such as toughness, threats of violence and homophobia do have an often negative impact on masculine identities, and the ways in which boys and men are positioned, this is not because masculinity itself is toxic, but because of the socio-political contexts in which they live. Michael Salter (2019) explained that:

> Connell and others theorized that common masculine ideals such as social respect, physical strength, and sexual potency become problematic when they set unattainable standards. Falling short can make boys and men insecure and anxious, which might prompt them to use force in order to feel, and be seen as, dominant and in control. Male violence in this scenario doesn't emanate from something bad or toxic that has crept into the nature of masculinity itself. Rather, it comes from these men's social and political settings, the particularities of which set them up for inner conflicts over social expectations and male entitlement.

It is, therefore, particular practices, rather than boys and men themselves, that are problematic (de Boise, 2019).

At the same time as notions of toxic masculinity have gained ground, gender relations are changing in many societies with both the disruption of gender binaries as trans and intersex become increasingly recognised and as the importance of gender equality has gained greater acknowledgement. As discussed in Chapter 1, some researchers suggest that there is also a new, and more inclusive version of masculinity among young men (Anderson, 2009). These issues, of how we understand gender equality, are not only individual ones but are deeply structured into societies.

The intense public debate about masculinity fits with some of the commonplaces from research on boys, men and masculinity. First, it shows the plurality of the ways in which masculinities are expressed within, and between, societies, with potentially different outcomes for all genders and society. Second, it indicates that masculinities are dynamic, changing over time (as well as across place) and, third, its features are contradictory, simultaneously stereotypically hegemonic and more inclusive; dominant and less powerful. These contradictions are partly between men and boys and sometimes embodied in one person.

Given the differences, dynamism and contradictions encapsulated in the notion of masculinities, it is important not to essentialise the concept. Some of the work to complexify thinking about masculinities has been produced in engagement with the ways in which hegemonic masculinities are theorised and some in attempts to recognise the transnational nature of masculinities as well as differences across countries. Jeff Hearn (2019) argued that it is crucial to consider the lives and practices of real men and boys, rather than treating theoretical constructs such as hegemonic masculinity as explaining particular boys' and men's lives and versions of masculinity. In other words, it is important not to treat masculinity as either a biological given or a character attribute. From within the field of Critical Studies on Men and Masculinities, Sam de Boise (2019) suggested that, 'rather than separating toxic from non-toxic masculinities, this requires a sensitivity to the potential implications of how the interplay of history, biography, discourse and geopolitics might be better integrated into our own conceptual frameworks rather than falling too easily into ready-made typologies which provide reductive answers to wider problems'.

## Nuancing Young Masculinities

This book has sought to de-essentialise and so nuance understandings of young masculinities by analysing the narratives of young people living in Helsinki. In doing so, it contributes to the relatively sparse literature on masculinities and boyhood outside the (predominantly) English-speaking world (Langa, 2020) by examining how boys negotiate masculinities in the multiple contexts in which they are positioned, including school, home and their hobbies. It does so theoretically by viewing masculinities as both intersectional and performative. Intersectionally, it recognises that the young people are all multiply positioned in social categories that also intersect with social structures. Performatively, it addresses masculinities as produced in everyday repetitive practices accessed through focus group discussions, individual interviews and photo-elicitation.

The chapters above apply these theoretical frames in four ways. First, they consider the ways in which boys from a variety of ethnicised groups negotiate masculinities in the different socio-economic spaces and places they move between in their everyday lives and over time, such as home, school, at their hobbies and in their geographical spheres. Second, as well as analysing the boys' narratives, the book considers the narratives of the few girls who agreed to take part in the study, showing how masculinities are relational in practice. Third, it analyses the young people's accounts of different aspects of their everyday practices such as joking, engagement with schoolwork, gaming and hobbies. Fourth, it examines masculinities as negotiated in different social relations (in individual interviews and focus group discussions), with parents, siblings, other boys and girls and through responses to representations of masculinities. The narratives that inform the book are, therefore, multi-sited as well as relational.

The findings generate insights into the social organisation of participants' lives and relations and the meanings they attribute to being masculine, as well as how they think about femininities. The findings provide new answers to the long-standing question of the continuing utility of the notion of hegemonic masculinities. Each of the empirical chapters above throws some light on this question and shows that the boys and girls in the study were in concert in emphasising differences between girls and boys that many treated in essentialist ways. Being a boy was, therefore, constructed as different from being a girl. The boys espoused a 'different but equal' ideology that fits with Finnish national norms. However, the ways in which they talked about girls established boys as superior. They also reported that 'gay' was among the most common forms of abuse at school. They denied that this was homophobic and sometimes said that homophobia was silly but, as in other studies, employed it in ways that reinforced heterosexual norms.

Boys were reported to be more likely to fight, including play fighting, than girls, but, unlike the findings from many other studies, including in Finland, they did not valorise toughness and threats of violence. In talking about gaming – something they considered differentiated boys from girls – they were often at pains to explain that, while they liked fighting and killing games, it was not because of the violence. The boys who were identified as popular were sometimes considered to have acquired fame because they were disruptive, but not identified as tough. Why might it be that this study did not find the propensity for violence reported by, for example, Manninen, Huuki and Sunnari (2011)? One reason may be that we did not ask directly about violence and the boys in the study did not spontaneously mention it. It may also be to do with place and time. Our study was done in Helsinki in the late 2010s, while Manninen and colleagues' study was conducted in more northern parts of Finland and at the beginning of the millennium. A larger-scale study asking directly about violence may have tapped into these issues in a different way. It is, however, clear from our findings that many Helsinki boys distance themselves from practices related to violence and the use of violence to establish or maintain dominance over other boys.

It is perhaps more surprising that most boys said that they did not want to be among the most popular boys because they viewed this as requiring boys to behave in ways that they did not aspire to act. This does not accord with notions that hegemonic masculinity organises the behaviour of men and boys because they aspire to attaining its characteristics. Instead, the boys in this study aspired to maintaining their difference from girls. The maintenance of differences from girls was one of the organising features of boys' understanding of their masculinities. This included in relation to schoolwork, but, whereas many studies (including our own) have found that part of hegemonic masculinity entails not being seen to do schoolwork, this was not a feature of the narratives of boys in this study. However, in keeping with other studies, some considered that girls worked so hard that they did badly and got easily upset at school, whereas boys did not work so hard and did well. They therefore nuanced the ways in which they maintained differences from girls in relation to schoolwork.

An equally important feature of boys' accounts was that they were friends with all boys (although some mentioned closer friends) and that joking relationships were central to masculinities. Yet, while boys were uniformly expected to be able to take jokes, it was clear to all that they should not be the butt of jokes. This very much fits with the findings of other studies, as does the racialisation of friendships (in schools that were sufficiently ethnically mixed for this to be relevant). That racialisation was geographically specific in that, unlike studies in the UK and the USA where black boys are considered particularly hegemonic, boys from minoritised ethnic groups were not admired. Although the boys' discourses were of ethnicised and racialised equality or colour-blindness, their narratives indicated that racist episodes were taken for granted. The few black boys in the study did not name racism, but a girl and trans boy interviewed together argued that white, middle-class boys were particularly exclusionary and racist.

One element of the notion of 'toxic masculinity' is that boys and men neither show emotion nor empathise with other people's emotions. Gilligan and Richards (2018) suggested that, within the codes of patriarchal masculinity, boys' need for supportive relationships comes to be seen as unmanly and subjected to shaming. In this study, boys generally agreed that, in comparison with girls, boys do not show emotion. Some boys considered that boys should be free to cry, but, in general, they considered that boys should only cry for the most major and painful reasons, such as the death of a loved one. In this, they again differentiated themselves from girls, whom they considered both emotional and able to confide in their friends. Their discussion of this sometimes sounded as if they considered this an unfair advantage accorded to girls. This reflected the more general tendency of some boys (and girls) to explicitly criticise the expectations related to hegemonic masculinities and to viewing boys and men as 'hard' while remaining attached to those expectations when talking about their everyday actions or values. In relation to the question of whether or not masculinities are changing in a more inclusive direction, this is perhaps an indication that masculinities may be changing to some extent, but that everyday practices are more resistant to change, or lag behind narrative claims. Whatever the processes involved, it was clear that boys generally did not confide in anyone. Many said that they could confide in their parents if need be but, as they got older, no longer did because, if they were to do so, it would implicate other boys who did not want parents told about anything they did.

While their narratives fitted to some extent with notions of hegemonic masculinities, the boys in this study did not aspire to hegemony. It was not simply that most recognised that they could not embody hegemonic masculinity (as, for example, found by Frosh et al., 2002), but that they also considered it unattractively costly to aspire to it in terms of, for example, being somewhat disruptive at school. Equally, they did claim differentiated versions of hegemony as has been reported in some studies (Connell, 2020). Instead, they seemed to desire to be similar enough to other boys not to stand out as different, while carefully avoiding being viewed as similar to girls. These two desires involved elements that would be recognised as hegemonic and involved power relations that created hierarchies in which boys considered themselves of higher status than girls and sometimes gay boys. However, it underlined the importance of considering actual boys' lives, rather than taking for granted that particular patterns of behaviour exemplify hegemonic masculinities (see Hearn et al., 2012). Perhaps not surprisingly, given the ways in which notions of hegemonic masculinity position girls as inferior, the few girls interviewed were more concerned with resisting and disrupting perspectives that could be considered emblematic of hegemonic masculinity, such as their exclusion from the forms of gaming boys valued.

## Processes of Crafting Liveable Lives Through Masculinities and Gender Relations

The pattern of the findings makes the importance of recognising gendered processes evident and lends some support to reformulations of 'hegemonic masculinities' (Connell, 2020; Hearn et al., 2012; Messerschmidt, 2018, 2019). In particular, they illuminate five sets of issues that have to be considered in studies and theorisations that seek to take holistic views of masculinities. First, the findings underline the importance of relationality in addressing gender (Connell, 1996, 2016). The boys' narratives indicated that they are different with girls than they are with boys, that they do different things with their mothers and fathers and that racialisation makes a difference to how they do masculinities. A few indicated that they were able to be different with close friends. Different versions of masculinities were, therefore, produced in relation to different people.

Second, place matters. To some extent, this is because different people are to be found in different places. Parents and siblings, for example, inhabit homes, while different groups of peers are interacted with in schools and hobbies. It is also because geographical specificities are produced from different histories that produce different ideologies (Hearn, 2015; Langa, 2020). As discussed in Chapter 1, Finland has its own normative ideologies of gender equality that could be seen in the boys' narratives. They also lived in the capital, Helsinki, and so cannot be assumed to be equivalent to boys from elsewhere in the country and the three schools in the study were selected because they differed in ethnic composition, which made a difference to the ways in which they boys constructed the intersections of racialisation and masculinities (see Chapter 8). Finland itself has specific histories in relation to colonisation, migration and racialisation that have made it newly conscious of itself as a multi-ethnic nation.

Third, temporality makes a difference, both because Finland itself is (as are all countries) dynamic in particular ways and because the young people themselves highlighted changes with age. For example, the older boys were beginning to see that some of their friends (and a few of those interviewed) were becoming interested in spending time with girls and beginning to negotiate ways in which to do this. Equally striking, as discussed above, they shifted their positioning in relation to their parents over time, with many explaining that they preferred to spend time with their peers than with their parents as they grew older.

Fourth, intersectionality was relevant to all the findings. While, for example, there were few black boys in the study, black boys were positioned differently from white Finnish boys in the young people's narratives – masculinities and ethnicities were inextricably linked. Social class played a role in organising hierarchies of masculine popularity through possibilities for consumption and informed boys' experiences, leisure practices and the distinctions they made (Bourdieu, 1984). Equally, the few girls in the study had different orientations to masculinities from the boys' orientations. There were no essentialist divisions between these groups, and this relates to the fifth way in which processes were visible in the findings: complexity, plurality and particularity were all equally important. Multiple, intersecting processes were, therefore, at play in the Helsinki schools, in ways that produce aspects of masculinities that are globally recognisable, but also specific to masculinities in Helsinki. Putting these issues together, it is clearly important to take a systemic view that recognises and analyses the dynamic processes produced through relationality, temporality, geographical specificity, intersectionality and complexity and particularity.

Overall, as would be expected from the many critical engagements with, and reformulation of, the notion of hegemonic masculinities, the analysis of the participants' narratives showed that the notion continues to have resonance for boys' everyday practices, but in complex, locally negotiated ways particular to contemporary Helsinki. This did not mean, however, that the boys instead espoused notions that fitted with the concept of inclusive masculinity – a concept that had little resonance in the three schools studied here. It may be that there is evidence of change in an inclusive direction. For example, one participant was overtly trans and he and the young woman with whom he was interviewed eschewed essentialist binary notions of gender. While they told about exclusionary practices that they had faced in school and other areas of life, they had a circle of friends who shared their understanding of gender as fluid and had managed to carve a social space for themselves amid the heteronormative order of the school. In addition, it was commonplace that participants espoused gender equality in ways consistent with contemporary Finnish ideologies. However, boys' narratives of gender seemed rather more conservative and contradictory than is predicted by theorisations of inclusive masculinity. Similar conclusions were reached in an Australian study of homosocial intimacy conducted with five focus groups (with 22 young men) and eight individual interviews (Ralph and Roberts, 2018: 100):

> Our research aimed to provide a deeper understanding of how young Australian men engage with what constitutes acceptable forms of homosocial intimacy. Although it is clear these young men are engaging in more physically and, in some cases, emotionally intimate friendships, the meanings attached to these behaviors do not squarely correspond with IMT [Inclusive Masculinity Theory](…) nor did their enactment of masculinity fit neatly with any of the field's primary theoretical frameworks. Instead, our participants' homosocial practices form part of a transitional step away from orthodox masculinity and toward genuinely changed gender relations. (…) While insufficient progress, this transitory phase should not be dismissed. Instead, we must continue to interrogate it to expose its contradictions and push toward inclusive masculinities and more equal gender relations.

Our findings indicate that the younger Finnish boys and girls in the study were in the process of negotiating and nuancing masculinities in different sites and with different people in ways that are globally recognisable, but simultaneously inflected with Finnish norms. As Langa (2020: 14) suggested from his research in South Africa, hegemonic masculinity is characterised by a 'constant process of negotiation, translation and reconfiguration in order to adapt to new historical periods and contexts'. The meanings that the young people made from their gendered, racialised practices were part of the process of crafting liveable, intersectional masculinities, femininities and gender relations in the context of normative expectations (Butler, 2004).

The young people in this study illuminated ways in which boyhood and masculinities are complex, diverse, dynamic, international and local in consonant and contradictory ways. As a whole, the book indicates that binaries such as inclusive versus hegemonic masculinity obscure, rather than illuminate the complex processes through which boys actively negotiate intersectional practices of masculinities in contemporary, multi-ethnic Helsinki.

# References


Aaltonen, S., A. Kivijärvi, M. Peltola and T. Tolonen. 2011. 'Ystävyydet'. In *Annettu, otettu, itse tehty. Nuorten vapaa-aika tänään*, edited by M. Määttä and T. Tolonen, 29–56. Helsinki: Nuorisotutkimusseura.

Aapola, S. 1999. *Murrosikä ja sukupuoli. Julkiset ja yksityiset ikämäärittelyt*. Helsinki: The Finnish Literature Society.

Adler, P. A., S. J. Kless and P. Adler. 1992. 'Socialization to Gender Roles: Popularity among Elementary School Boys and Girls'. *Sociology of Education* 65(3): 169–87. https://doi.org/10.2307/2112807.

Alemanji, A. A. 2016. *Is There Such a Thing...?: A Study of Antiracism Education in Finland*. Helsinki: University of Helsinki.

Alemanji, A. A. and F. Dervin. 2016. '"If an Apple Is a Foreign Apple You Have to Wash It Very Carefully": Youth Discourses on Racism'. *Education, Citizenship and Social Justice* 11(3): 199–212. https://doi.org/10.1177/1746197916648284.

Allan, J. A. 2018. 'Masculinity as Cruel Optimism'. *NORMA International Journal for Masculinity Studies* 13(3–4): 175–90. https://doi.org/10.1080/18902138.2017.1312949.

Allen, L. 2005. 'Managing Masculinity: Young Men's Identity Work in Focus Groups'. *Qualitative Research* 5(1): 35–57. https://doi.org/10.1177/1468794105048650.

American Psychological Association, Boys and Men Guidelines Group. 2018a. 'APA Guidelines for Psychological Practice with Boys and Men'. Accessed 5 January 2021. http://www.apa.org/about/policy/psychological-practice-boys-men-guidelines.pdf.

American Psychological Association, Boys and Men Guidelines Group. 2018b. 'Harmful Masculinity and Violence: Understanding the Connection and Approaches to Prevention'. Accessed 5 January 2021. https://www.apa.org/pi/about/newsletter/2018/09/harmful-masculinity.

Anderson, E. 2009. *Inclusive Masculinity: The Changing Nature of Masculinities*. London: Routledge.

Anderson, E. 2018. 'Generational Masculinities'. *Journal of Gender Studies* 27(3): 243–47. https://doi.org/10.1080/09589236.2017.1406088.

Anderson, E. and M. McCormack. 2018. 'Inclusive Masculinity Theory: Overview, Reflection and Refinement'. *Journal of Gender Studies* 27(5): 547–61. https://doi.org/10.1080/09589236.2016.1245605.

Anthias, F. 2020. *Translocational Belongings: Intersectional Dilemmas and Social Inequalities*. London: Routledge.

Armila, P., M. Käyhkö and V. Pöysä. 2018. 'Syrjäkylien pojat: Kaveruutta ja kilometrejä'. In *Poikatutkimus*, edited by A. Kivijärvi, T. Huuki and H. Lunabba, 261–86. Tampere: Vastapaino.

Arnesen, A. L., E. Lahelma and E. Öhrn. 2008. 'Travelling Discourses on Gender and Education. The Case of Boys' Underachievement'. *Nordisk Pedagogik* 28: 1–14.

Attwood, F. 2007. 'Sluts and Riot Grrrls: Female Identity and Sexual Agency'. *Journal of Gender Studies* 16(3): 233–247. https://doi.org/10.1080/09589230701562921.

Bamberg, M. 2004. 'Form and Functions of "Slut Bashing" in Male Identity Constructions in 15-Year-Olds'. *Human Development* 47(6): 331–53. https://doi.org/10.1159/000081036.

Barbour, R. 2018. *Doing Focus Groups*. London: Sage.

Barnes, C. 2012. 'It's No Laughing Matter… Boys' Humour and the Performance of Defensive Masculinities in the Classroom'. *Journal of Gender Studies* 21(3): 239–51. https://doi.org/10.1080/09589236.2012.691648.

Bastos, R. M. B. 2017. 'The Surprising Success of the Finnish Educational System in a Global Scenario of Commodified Education'. *Revista Brasileira de Educação*, 22: 802–25. https://doi.org/10.1590/S1413-24782017227040.

Beasley, C. 2013. 'Rethinking Hegemonic Masculinity in Transnational Context'. In *Rethinking Transnational Men: Beyond, Between and*

*Within Nations*, edited by J. Hearn and K. Harrison, 29–44. London: Routledge.

Bell, D. 2013. 'Geek Myths: Technologies, Masculinities, Globalizations'. In *Rethinking Transnational Men*, edited by J. Hearn, M. Blagojević and K. Harrison, 92–106. London: Routledge.

Berg, P. and M. Peltola. 2015. 'Raising Decent Citizens. On Respectability, Parenthood and Drawing Boundaries'. *NORA – Nordic Journal of Feminist and Gender Research* 23(1): 36–51. https://doi.org/10.1080/08038740.2014.938116.

Berlant, L. 2010. 'Cruel Optimism'. In *The Affect Theory Reader*, edited by M. Gregg and G. J. Seigworth. Durham, NC: Duke University Press. https://doi.org/10.1515/9780822393047.

Bernelius, V. and M. Vaattovaara. 2016. 'Choice and Segregation in the "Most Egalitarian" Schools: Cumulative Decline in Urban Schools and Neighbourhoods of Helsinki, Finland'. *Urban Studies* 53(15): 3155–71. https://doi.org/10.1177/0042098015621441.

Bhana, D. and E. Mayeza. 2019. '"Cheese Boys" Resisting and Negotiating Violent Hegemonic Masculinity in Primary School'. *NORMA* 14(1): 3–17. https://doi.org/10.1080/18902138.2018.1494402.

Bonilla-Silva, E. and D. Dietrich. 2011. 'The Sweet Enchantment of Color-Blind Racism in Obamerica'. *The Annals of the American Academy of Political and Social Science* 634(1): 190–206. https://doi.org/10.1177/0002716210389702.

Bourdieu, P. 1984. *Distinction. A Social Critique of the Judgement of Taste*. Cambridge, MA: Harvard University Press.

Brah, A. and A. Phoenix. 2004. 'Ain't I a Woman? Revisiting Intersectionality'. *Journal of International Women's Studies* 5(3): 75–86. https://vc.bridgew.edu/jiws/vol5/iss3/8.

Bridges, T. and C. J. Pascoe. 2014. 'Hybrid Masculinities: New Directions in the Sociology of Men and Masculinities'. *Sociology Compass* 8(3): 246–58. https://doi.org/10.1111/soc4.12134.

Bruner, J. 1990. *Acts of Meaning*. Cambridge, MA: Harvard University Press.

Bruner, J. S. 2003. *Making Stories: Law, Literature, Life*. Cambridge, MA: Harvard University Press.

Bryan, N. 2020. 'Shaking the Bad Boys: Troubling the Criminalization of Black Boys' Childhood Play, Hegemonic White Masculinity and Femininity, and the School Playground-to-Prison Pipeline'. *Race Ethnicity and Education* 23(5): 673–92. https://doi.org/10.1080/13613324.2018.1512483.

Burgos, M. 1991. 'Analysing Texts' Workshop. Thomas Coram Research Unit, Resources within Households Study Group, coordinated by Julia Brannen and Gail Wilson.

Burrell, S. and S. Ruxton. 2020. 'Coronavirus Reveals Just How Deep Macho Stereotypes Run through Society'. Accessed 8 March 2020. https://theconversation.com/coronavirus-reveals-just-how-deep-macho-stereotypes-run-through-society-134968.

Butler, J. 1990. *Gender Trouble. Feminism and the Subversion of Identity.* New York: Routledge.

Butler, J. 2004. *Undoing Gender*. New York: Routledge.

Cann, V., S. Madrid, K. Ratele, A. Tarrant, M. R. M. Ward and R. Connell. 2021. 'The Men and the Boys, Twenty Years On: Revisiting Raewyn Connell's Pivotal Text'. *Boyhood Studies* 14(1): 1–5. https://doi.org/10.3167/bhs.2021.140101.

Carrigan, T., B. Connell and J. Lee. 1985. 'Toward a New Sociology of Masculinity'. *Theory and Society* 14(5): 551–604. https://doi.org/10.1007/BF00160017.

Castrén, A-M. and K. Ketokivi. 2015. 'Studying the Complex Dynamics of Family Relationships: A Figurational Approach'. *Sociological Research Online* 20(1): [3]. https://doi.org/10.5153/sro.3539.

Cawie, C. and S. Lees. 1981. 'Slags or Drags'. *Feminist Review* 9(1): 17–31. https://doi.org/10.1057/fr.1981.17.

Christensen, A-D. and S. Q. Jensen. 2014. 'Combining Hegemonic Masculinity and Intersectionality'. *NORMA International Journal for Masculinity Studies* 9(1): 60–75. https://doi.org/10.1080/18902138.2014.892289.

Clark-Ibáñez, M. 2004. 'Framing the Social World with Photo-Elicitation Interviews'. *American Behavioral Scientist* 47(12): 1507–27. https://doi.org/10.1177/0002764204266236.

Collins, P. H. and S. Bilge. 2020. *Intersectionality*. Cambridge: Polity.

Connell, R. W. 1989. 'Cool Guys, Swots and Wimps: The Interplay of Masculinity and Education'. *Oxford Review of Education* 15(3): 291–303. https://doi.org/10.1080/0305498890150309.

Connell, R. W. 1995 [1987]. *Masculinities*. Berkeley, CA: University of California Press.

Connell, R. W. 1996. 'Teaching the Boys: New Research on Masculinity, and Gender Strategies for Schools'. *Teachers College Record* 98(2): 206–35. https://psycnet.apa.org/record/1997-07468-001.

Connell, R. W. 1998. 'Masculinities and Globalization'. *Men and Masculinities* 1(1): 3–23. https://doi.org/10.1177/1097184X98001001001.

Connell, R. 2016. 'Masculinities in Global Perspective: Hegemony, Contestation, and Changing Structures of Power'. *Theory and Society* 45(4): 303–18. https://www.jstor.org/stable/44981834.

Connell, R. 2020. 'Making the Men and the Boys'. *Boyhood Studies* 13(2): 9–19. https://doi.org/10.3167/bhs.2020.130202.

Connell, R. 2021. *Gender: In World Perspective*. 4th ed. Cambridge: Polity.

Connell, R. W. and J. W. Messerschmidt. 2005. 'Hegemonic Masculinity: Rethinking the Concept'. *Gender and Society* 19(6): 829–59. https://doi.org/10.1177/0891243205278639.

Cooper, V. L. 2017. 'Lost in Translation: Exploring Childhood Identity using Photo-Elicitation'. *Children's Geographies* 15(6): 625–37. https://doi.org/10.1080/14733285.2017.1284306.

Cornwall, A. and N. Lindisfarne, eds. 1995. *Dislocating Masculinity: Comparative Ethnographies*. London: Taylor & Francis.

Crenshaw, K. W. 2017. *On Intersectionality: Essential Writings*. New York: The New Press.

Crenshaw, K. W. 2020. 'The Unmattering of Black Lives'. *The New Republic*. Accessed 5 January 2021. https://newrepublic.com/article/157769/unmattering-black-lives.

Croghan, R., C. Griffin, J. Hunter and A. Phoenix. 2008. 'Young People's Constructions of Self: Notes on the Use and Analysis of the Photo-Elicitation Methods'. *International Journal of Social Research Methodology* 11(4): 345–56. https://doi.org/10.1080/13645570701605707.

Davies, K. 2015. 'Siblings, Stories and the Self: The Sociological Significance of Young People's Sibling Relationships'. *Sociology* 49(4): 679–95. https://doi.org/10.1177/0038038514551091.

de Boise, S. 2019. 'Editorial: Is Masculinity Toxic?' *NORMA International Journal for Masculinity Studies* 14(3): 147–51. https://doi.org/10.1080/18902138.2019.1654742.

de Boise, S. 2018. 'The Personal Is Political… Just Not Always Progressive: Affective Interruptions and Their Promise for CSMM'. *NORMA International Journal for Masculinity Studies* 13(3–4): 158–74. https://doi.org/10.1080/18902138.2017.1325098

de Boise, S. and J. Hearn. 2017. 'Are Men Getting More Emotional? Critical Sociological Perspectives on Men, Masculinities and Emotions'. *The Sociological Review* 65(4): 779–96. https://doi.org/10.1177/0038026116686500.

Del Aguila, E. V. 2013. *Being a Man in a Transnational World: The Masculinity and Sexuality of Migration*. New York: Routledge.

Demetriou, D. Z. 2001. 'Connell's Concept of Hegemonic Masculinity: A Critique'. *Theory and Society* 30(3): 337–61. https://doi.org/10.1023/A:1017596718715.

Deuchar, R. and G. Goulden. 2020. 'Coronavirus: Pressure on Boys "to Be a Man Is Growing"'. Accessed 8 March 2020. https://www.tes.com/news/coronavirus-pressure-boys-be-man-growing.

Duffy, A. L., S. Penn, D. Nesdale and M. J. Zimmer-Gembeck. 2017. 'Popularity: Does It Magnify Associations between Popularity Prioritization and the Bullying and Defending Behavior of Early Adolescent Boys and Girls?' *Social Development* 26(2): 263–77. https://doi.org/10.1111/sode.12206.

Edley, N. and M. Wetherell. 1995. *Men in Perspective*. London: Pearson Education Limited.

Edwards, R., L. Hadfield, H. Lucey and M. Mauthner. 2006. *Sibling Identity and Relationships: Sisters and Brothers*. London: Routledge.

Edwards, T. 2004. *Cultures of Masculinity*. New York: Routledge.

Eerola, P. 2014. 'Maskuliinisuuden myötä- ja vastakerronta haastattelupuheessa'. *Sukupuolentutkimus* 27(2): 31–44.

Eerola, P. and J. Huttunen. 2011. 'Metanarrative of the "New Father" and Narratives of Young Finnish First-Time Fathers'. *Fathering* 9(3): 211–31. https://doi.org/10.3149/fth.0903.211.

Elliott, K. 2016. 'Caring Masculinities: Theorizing an Emergent Concept'. *Men and Masculinities* 19(3): 240–59. https://doi.org/10.1177/1097184X15576203.

Elliott, K. and S. Roberts. 2020. 'Balancing Generosity and Critique: Reflections on Interviewing Young Men and Implications for Research Methodologies and Ethics'. *Qualitative Research* 20(6): 767–83. https://doi.org/10.1177/1468794120904881.

Erola, J., ed. 2010. *Luokaton Suomi? Yhteiskuntaluokat 2000-luvun Suomessa*. Helsinki: Gaudeamus.

European Commission. 2021. *2021 Report on Gender Equality in the EU*. Luxembourg: Publications Office of the European Union. 2021 Report on Gender Equality in the EU (europa.eu).

Fanon, F. 1967. *Black Skin, White Masks*. New York: Grove Press.

Fergus, E. and J. Bennett. 2018. 'Introduction: Masculinity and Boyhood Constructions in the School-to-Prison Pipeline'. *Boyhood Studies* 11(2): 1–16. https://doi.org/10.3167/bhs.2018.110201.

Ferguson, A. A. 2000. *Bad Boys. Public Schools in the Making of Black Masculinity*. Ann Arbor, MI: University of Michigan Press.

Finnish Institute for Health and Welfare. 2021. 'Koulutuksen sukupuolen mukainen segregaatio'. Accessed 10 June 2021. https://thl.fi/fi/web/sukupuolten-tasa-arvo/tasa-arvon-tila/koulutus-ja-kasvatus/koulutuksen-sukupuolen-mukainen-segregaatio.

Flood, M. 2018. 'Toxic Masculinity: A Primer and Commentary'. *XY: Men, Masculinities, and Gender Politics*, 7 June 2018. Accessed 28 July 2020. https://xyonline.net/content/toxic-masculinity-primer-and-commentary.

Foucault, M. 1977. *Discipline and Punish: The Birth of the Prison*. New York: Pantheon.

Francis, D. A. and J. I. Kjaran. 2020. 'Troubling the Discourse of the Victimization of Queer Youth in Icelandic and South African Education'. *Feminism & Psychology* 30(4): 425–44. https://doi.org/10.1177/0959353520912960.

Frosh, S., A. Phoenix and R. Pattman. 2002. *Young Masculinities: Understanding Boys in Contemporary Society*. London: Macmillan.

Gillies, V. and H. Lucey. 2006. '"It's a Connection You Can't Get Away From": Brothers, Sisters and Social Capital'. *Journal of Youth Studies* 9(4): 479–93. https://doi.org/10.1080/13676260600914549.

Gilligan, C. and D. A. Richards. 2018. *Darkness Now Visible: Patriarchy's Resurgence and Feminist Resistance*. Cambridge: Cambridge University Press.

Ging, D. 2019. 'Alphas, Betas, and Incels: Theorizing the Masculinities of the Manosphere'. *Men and Masculinities* 22(4): 638–57. https://doi.org/10.1177/1097184X17706401.

Glick, P. 2020. 'Masks and Emasculation: Why Some Men Refuse to Take Safety Precautions'. *Scientific American*, 30 April. Accessed 5 January 2021. https://blogs.scientificamerican.com/observations/masks-and-emasculation-why-some-men-refuse-to-take-safety-precautions.

Gordon, A. F., K. Hite and D. Jara. 2020. 'Haunting and Thinking from the Utopian Margins: Conversation with Avery Gordon'. *Memory Studies* 13(3): 337–46. https://doi.org/10.1177/1750698020914017.

Gordon, T., J. Holland and E. Lahelma. 2000. *Making Spaces: Citizenship and Difference in Schools*. London: Palgrave Macmillan.

Gottzén, L., U. Mellström and T. Shefer, eds. 2019. *Routledge International Handbook of Masculinity Studies*. London: Routledge.

Gough, B., K. Milnes and T. Turner-Moore. 2019. 'Young Masculinities across Five European Countries: Performing under Pressure'. *Journal of Youth Studies* 24(1): 77–90. https://doi.org/10.1080/13676261.2019.1695763.

Gracia, P., J. Garcia-Roman, T. Oinas and T. Anttila. 2020. 'Do Boys' and Girls' Daily Activities Differ? Cross-Country Evidence'. *SocArXiv*. Accessed 5 January 2021. https://osf.io/preprints/socarxiv/nruq7.

Gramsci, A. 1971. *Selections from the Prison Notebooks*. Edited and translated by Q. Hoare and G.N. Smith. London: Lawrence & Wishart.

Gross, C., A. Gottburgsen and A. Phoenix. 2016. 'Education Systems and Intersectionality'. *Education Systems and Inequalities: International Comparisons*, edited by A. Hadjar and C. Gross, 51–72. https://doi.org/10.1332/policypress/9781447326106.003.0004.

Gubrium, A. 2006. '"I Was My Momma Baby. I Was My Daddy Gal": Strategic Stories of Success'. *Narrative Inquiry* 16(2): 231–53. https://doi.org/10.1075/ni.16.2.02gub.

Gunaratnam, Y. 2003. *Researching 'Race' and Ethnicity: Methods, Knowledge and Power*. London: Sage.

Hakanen, T., S. Myllyniemi and M. Salasuo. 2018. *Oikeus liikkua. Lasten ja nuorten vapaa-aikatutkimus 2018*. Helsinki: Opetus- ja kulttuuriministeriö, Valtion liikuntaneuvosto, Valtion nuorisoneuvosto & Nuorisotutkimusseura.

Hall, J. J. 2020. '"The Word Gay Has Been Banned but People Use It in the Boys' Toilets Whenever You Go in": Spatialising Children's Subjectivities in Response to Gender and Sexualities Education in English Primary Schools'. *Social & Cultural Geography* 21(2): 162–85. https://doi.org/10.1080/14649365.2018.1474377.

Halme, N., L. Hedman, R. Ikonen and R. Rajala. 2018. *Lasten ja nuorten hyvinvointi 2017. Kouluterveyskyselyn tuloksia*. Helsinki: Finnish Institute of Health and Welfare.

Harinen, P., V. Honkasalo, J. Ronkainen and L. Suurpää. 2012. 'Multiculturalism and Young People's Leisure Spaces in Finland: Perspectives of Multicultural Youth'. *Leisure Studies* 31(2): 177–91. https://doi.org/10.1080/02614367.2011.576427.

Harper, D. 2002. 'Talking about Pictures: A Case for Photo Elicitation'. *Visual Studies* 17(1): 13–26. https://doi.org/10.1080/14725860220137345.

Harvey, L., J. Ringrose and R. Gill. 2013. 'Swagger, Ratings and Masculinity: Theorising the Circulation of Social and Cultural Value in Teenage Boys' Digital Peer Networks'. *Sociological Research Online* 18(4): 57–67. https://doi.org/10.5153/sro.3153.

Haywood, C., T. Johansson, N. Hammarén, M. Herz and A. Ottemo. 2018. *The Conundrum of Masculinity: Hegemony, Homosociality, Homophobia and Heteronormativity*. London: Routledge.

Hearn, J. 2004. 'From Hegemonic Masculinity to the Hegemony of Men'. *Feminist Theory* 5(1): 49–72. https://doi.org/10.1177/1464700104040813.

Hearn, J. 2015. 'Transnational Reflections on Transnational Research Projects on Men, Boys and Gender Relations'. *NORMA International Journal for Masculinity Studies* 10(2): 86–104. https://doi.org/10.1080/18902138.2015.1050858.

Hearn, J. 2019. 'So What Has Been, Is, and Might Be Going On in Studying Men and Masculinities? Some Continuities and Discontinuities'. *Men and Masculinities* 22(1): 53–63. https://doi.org/10.1177/1097184X18805550.

Hearn, J. and M. Blagojević. 2013. 'Introducing and Rethinking Transnational Men'. In *Rethinking Transnational Men: Beyond, Between and Within Nations*, edited by J. Hearn, M. Blagojević and K. Harrison. London: Routledge.

Hearn, J., M. Nordberg, K. Andersson, D. Balkmar, L. Gottzén, R. Klinth, K. Pringle and L. Sandberg. 2012. 'Hegemonic Masculinity and Beyond: 40 Years of Research in Sweden'. *Men and Masculinities* 15(1): 31–55. https://doi.org/10.1177/1097184X11432113.

Heyder, A. and U. Kessels. 2017. 'Boys Don't Work? On the Psychological Benefits of Showing Low Effort in High School'. *Sex Roles* 77 (1–2): 72–85. https://doi.org/10.1007/s11199-016-0683-1.

Hoikkala, T. and P. Paju. 2014. *Apina pulpetissa. Ysiluokan yhteisöllisyys*. Helsinki: Gaudeamus.

Holli, A. M. and J. Kantola. 2007. 'State Feminism Finnish Style: Strong Policies Clash with Implementation Problems'. In *Changing State Feminism*, edited by J. Outshoorn and J. Kantola. Basingstoke: Palgrave Macmillan.

Honkasalo, V. 2013. 'Save the Girls! Gender Equality and Multiculturalism in Finnish Youth Work Contexts'. *Journal of Girlhood Studies* 6(2): 47–64.

HS 10.11.2020. Helsingin keskustassa liikkuu nyt joukoissa yli sata mahdollisesti vaarallista nuorta – Asiantuntijoiden mukaan taustalla on uusi maahanmuuttoon liittyvä ilmiö. *Helsingin Sanomat*. Accessed 4 January 2021. https://www.hs.fi/kaupunki/art-2000007609651.html.

HS 18.12.2020. Uutta tietoa 16-vuotiaan surmasta Koskelassa: Poliisin mukaan taustalla on pitkään jatkunutta kiusaamista, epäillyt kävivät uhrin luona seuraavana päivänä. *Helsingin Sanomat.* Accessed 4 January 2021. https://www.hs.fi/kaupunki/art-2000007691111.html.

Huuki, T. 2010a. *Koulupoikien statustyö väkivallan ja välittämisen valokiilassa.* Oulu: University of Oulu.

Huuki, T. 2010b. 'Välittämisen vaikeus maskuliinisuuden rakentumisessa'. *Nuorisotutkimus* 28(1): 3–19.

Huuki, T., S. Manninen and V. Sunnari. 2010. 'Humour as a Resource and Strategy for Boys to Gain Status in the Field of Informal School'. *Gender and Education* 22(4): 369–83. https://doi.org/10.1080/09540250903352317.

Huuki, T. and V. Sunnari. 2015. 'Standing By... Standing Off – Troublesome Compassion in the Relationships of School Boys'. *Gender and Education* 27(5): 555–74. https://doi.org/10.1080/09540253.2015.1069798.

Hygen, B. W., J. Belsky, F. Stenseng, V. Skalicka, M. N. Kvande, T. Zahl-Thanem and L. Wichstrøm. 2020. 'Time Spent Gaming and Social Competence in Children: Reciprocal Effects across Childhood'. *Child Development* 91(3): 861–75. https://doi.org/10.1111/cdev.13243.

Hyvönen, H. 2020. 'Poststrukturalismi ja hegemoninen maskuliinisuus – hankala yhtälö kriittisen miestutkimuksen kentällä?' *Sukupuolentutkimus* 33(2): 46–53.

Ingram, N. 2018. *Working-Class Boys and Educational Success.* London: Palgrave Macmillan.

Janmaat, J. G. and A. Keating. 2019. 'Are Today's Youth More Tolerant? Trends in Tolerance among Young People in Britain'. *Ethnicities* 19(1): 44–65. https://doi.org/10.1177/1468796817723682.

Janssen, D. F. 2015. 'After Boyology, Or, Whence and Whither Boyhood Studies?' *Boyhood Studies* 8(1): 1–14. https://doi.org/10.3167/bhs.2015.080101.

Jenson, J. and S. de Castell. 2011. 'Girls@ Play: An Ethnographic Study of Gender and Digital Gameplay'. *Feminist Media Studies* 11(2): 167–79. https://doi.org/10.1080/14680777.2010.521625.

Julkunen, R. 2010. *Sukupuolen järjestykset ja tasa-arvon paradoksit.* Tampere: Vastapaino.

Kahma, N. 2010. 'Keskiluokan valossa. Suomalaisten luokkasamastuminen empiirisessä tarkastelussa'. *Sosiologia* 47(2): 81–96.

Kantola, J., O. C. Norocel and J. Repo. 2011. 'Gendering Violence in the School Shootings in Finland'. *European Journal of Women's Studies* 18(2): 183–97. https://doi.org/10.1177/1350506810394614.

Keddie, A. 2020. 'Engaging Boys and Young Men in Gender Transformation: The Possibilities and Limits of a Pedagogy of Empathy'. *NORMA 15*(2): 97–110. https://doi.org/10.1080/18902138.2019.1706883.

Keddie, A. 2021. 'Engaging Boys in Gender Activism: Issues of Discomfort and Emotion'. *Gender and Education* 33(2): 171–85. https://doi.org/10.1080/09540253.2020.1716956.

Kehily, M. J. and A. Nayak. 1997. '"Lads and Laughter": Humour and the Production of Heterosexual Hierarchies'. *Gender and Education* 9(1): 69–88. https://doi.org/10.1080/09540259721466.

Kendall, L. 1999. '"The Nerd Within": Mass Media and the Negotiation of Identity among Computer-Using Men'. *The Journal of Men's Studies* 7(3): 353–69.

Keskinen, S. 2018. 'The "Crisis" of White Hegemony, Neonationalist Femininities and Antiracist Feminism'. *Women's Studies International Forum* 68: 157–63. https://doi.org/10.1016/j.wsif.2017.11.001.

Keskinen, S., S. Tuori, S. Irni and D. Mulinari, D., eds. 2009. *Complying with Colonialism. Gender, Race and Ethnicity in the Nordic Region.* Farnham: Ashgate.

Kilpi-Jakonen, E. 2014. 'Citizenship and Educational Attainment amongst the Second Generation: An Analysis of Children of Immigrants in Finland'. *Journal of Ethnic and Migration Studies* 40(7): 1079–96. https://doi.org/10.1080/1369183X.2013.831543.

Kimanen, A. 2018. 'Approaching culture, negotiating practice: Finnish educators' discourses on cultural diversity'. *Journal of Multicultural Discourses* 13(4): 334–347. DOI: https://doi.org/10.1080/17447143.2018.1546309

Kimmel, M. 2017. 'Foreword'. In *Masculinity and Aspiration in an Era of Neoliberal Education: International Perspectives*, edited by G. Stahl, J. Nelson and D. Wallace. London: Routledge.

Kivijärvi, A., T. Huuki and H. Lunabba, eds. 2018. *Poikatutkimus.* Tampere: Vastapaino.

Kivinen, O., J. Hedman and P. Kaipainen. 2012. 'Koulutusmahdollisuuksien yhdenvertaisuus Suomessa. Eriarvoisuuden uudet ja vanhat muodot'. *Yhteiskuntapolitiikka* 77(5): 559–66.

Kolbe, L. 2010. 'Esipuhe: Luokat, myytit ja suuri kansallinen kertomus'. In *Luokaton Suomi? Yhteiskuntaluokat 2000-luvun Suomessa*, edited by J. Erola, 5–9. Helsinki: Gaudeamus.

Kondelin, S. 2016. 'Feminiinisyys, transmaskuliinisuus ja mieheys'. *Sukupuolentutkimus* 29(1): 53–56.

Kosonen, T. 2016. *Opiskeleva ammattimies, yhteiskuntaluokka ja sukupuoli. Tutkimus ammatilliseen aikuiskoulutukseen osallistuvista työläismiehistä*. Joensuu: University of Eastern Finland.

Kosunen, S. 2014. 'Reputation and Parental Logics of Action in Local School Choice Space in Finland'. *Journal of Education Policy* 29(4): 443–66. https://doi.org/10.1080/02680939.2013.844859.

Kosunen, S., V. Bernelius, P. Seppänen and M. Porkka. 2020. 'School Choice to Lower Secondary Schools and Mechanisms of Segregation in Urban Finland'. *Urban Education* 55(10): 1461–88. https://doi.org/10.1177/0042085916666933.

Kramer, A. S. and A. B. Harris. 2020. *Breaking Through Bias: Communication Techniques for Women to Succeed at Work*. London: Routledge.

Kurki, T. 2019. *Immigrant-ness as (Mis)fortune? Immigrantisation through Integration Policies and Practices in Education*. Helsinki: University of Helsinki.

Käyhkö, M. 2006. *Siivoojaksi oppimassa. Etnografinen tutkimus työläistytöistä puhdistuspalvelualan koulutuksessa*. Joensuu: Joensuu University Press.

Labov, W. 1969. 'The Logic of Non-standard English'. In *Georgetown Monograph on Languages and Linguistics 22*, edited by J. Atlantis, 1–44.

Lareau, A. 2003. *Unequal Childhoods. Class, Race, and Family Life*. Berkeley, CA: University of California.

Langa, M. 2020. *Becoming Men: Black Masculinities in a South African Township*. Johannesburg: Wits University Press.

Lee, S. J. 2004. 'Hmong American Masculinities: Creating New Identities in the United States'. In *Adolescent Boys: Exploring Diverse Cultures of Boyhood*, edited by N. Way and J. Y. Chu, 13–30. New York: New York University Press.

Lehtonen, J. 2002. *Seksuaalisuus ja sukupuoli koulussa. Näkökulmana heteronormatiivisuus ja ei-heteroseksuaalisten nuorten kertomukset*. Helsinki: Helsinki University Press.

Leonardo, Z. 2009. *Race, Whiteness, and Education*. Abingdon: Routledge.

Levesque, A. 2016. 'Rethinking Homophobia and Deviant Youth Masculinities: Constructing and Interrogating Progress toward Equality'. *Sociology Compass* 10(8): 643–51. https://doi.org/10.1111/soc4.12394.

Livingstone, S. 2009. *Children and the Internet: Great Expectations, Challenging Realities*. Cambridge: Polity.

Livingstone, S. and A. Blum-Ross. 2020. *Parenting for a Digital Future: How Hopes and Fears about Technology Shape Children's Lives*. Oxford: Oxford University Press.

Lobel, A., R. C. Engels, L. L. Stone, W. J. Burk and I. Granic. 2017. 'Video Gaming and Children's Psychosocial Wellbeing: A Longitudinal Study'. *Journal of Youth and Adolescence* 46(4): 884–97. https://doi.org/10.1007/s10964-017-0646-z.

Lucas, K. and J. L. Sherry. 2004. 'Sex Differences in Video Game Play: A Communication-Based Explanation'. *Communication Research* 31(5): 499–523. https://doi.org/10.1177/0093650204267930.

Lunabba, H. 2013. *När vuxna möter pojkar i skolan - insyn, inflytande och sociala relationer*. Helsinki: University of Helsinki.

Lunabba, H. 2018. 'Laadullisen tutkimuksen näkökulma poikien koulu- ja hyvinvointikeskusteluun'. In *Poikatutkimus*, edited by A. Kivijärvi, T. Huuki and H. Lunabba, 103–120. Tampere: Vastapaino.

Luttrell, W. 2020. *Children Framing Childhoods: Working-Class Kids' Visions of Care*. Cambridge: Policy Press.

Lutz, H. 2015. 'Intersectionality as Method'. *DiGeSt. Journal of Diversity and Gender Studies* 2(1–2): 39–44. https://www.jstor.org/stable/10.11116/jdivegendstud.2.1-2.0039.

Mac an Ghaill, M. and C. Haywood. 2014. 'Pakistani and Bangladeshi Young Men: Re-racialization, Class and Masculinity within the Neo-liberal School'. *British Journal of Sociology of Education* 35(5): 753–76. https://doi.org/10.1080/01425692.2014.919848.

Majors, R. and J. M. Billson. 1993. *Cool Pose: The Dilemma of Black Manhood in America*. New York: Simon & Schuster.

Mann, S. 2016. 'Qualitative Interviews Overview'. In *The Research Interview. Reflective Practice and Reflexivity in Research Processes*, edited by S. Mann, 30–57. London: Palgrave Macmillan.

Manninen, S. 2010. *'Iso, vahva, rohkee – kaikenlaista'. Maskuliinisuudet, poikien valtahierarkiat ja väkivalta koulussa*. Oulu: University of Oulu.

Manninen, S. 2013. 'Masculinity and Respect in Flux: Olli's Story'. *Gender and Education* 25(7): 872–88. https://doi.org/10.1080/09540253.2013.858109.

Manninen, S., T. Huuki and V. Sunnari. 2011. 'Earn yo'respect! Respect in the Status Struggle of Finnish School Boys'. *Men and Masculinities* 14(3): 335–57. https://doi.org/10.1177/1097184X10369476.

Martikainen, T., T. Sintonen and P. Pitkänen. 2006. 'Ylirajainen liikkuvuus ja etniset vähemmistöt'. In *Ylirajainen kulttuuri: Etnisyys*

*Suomessa 2000-luvulla*, edited by T. Martikainen, 9–41. Helsinki: Finnish Literature Society.

Martino, W. and M. Pallotta-Chiarolli. 2003. *So What's A Boy? Addressing Issues of Masculinity and Schooling*. Maidenhead: Open University Press.

Massey, D. 2005. *For Space*. London: Sage.

Maybin, J. 2013. 'Towards a Sociocultural Understanding of Children's Voice'. *Language and Education* 27(5): 383–97. https://doi.org/10.1080/09500782.2012.704048.

McCormack, M. 2011. 'Hierarchy without Hegemony: Locating Boys in an Inclusive Masculinity Setting'. *Sociological Perspectives* 54(1): 83–101. https://doi.org/10.1525/sop.2011.54.1.83.

McCormack, M. and E. Anderson. 2010. 'The re-production of homosexually-themed discourse in educationally-based organised sport'. *Culture, Health & Sexuality* 12(8): 913–27.

McDowell, L. 2012. 'Post-crisis, Post-Ford and Post-gender? Youth Identities in an Era of Austerity'. *Journal of Youth Studies* 15(5): 573–90. https://doi.org/10.1080/13676261.2012.671933.

Mesman, J. and M. G. Groeneveld. 2018. 'Gendered Parenting in Early Childhood: Subtle but Unmistakable if You Know Where to Look'. *Child Development Perspectives* 12(1): 22–27. https://doi.org/10.1111/cdep.12250.

Messerschmidt, J. W. 2018. *Hegemonic Masculinity: Formulation, Reformulation, and Amplification*. Lanham, MD: Rowman & Littlefield.

Messerschmidt, J. W. 2019. 'The Salience of "Hegemonic Masculinity"'. *Men and Masculinities* 22(1): 85–91. https://doi.org/10.1177/1097184X18805555.

Ministry of Education and Culture. 2020. *Comprehensive School*. Helsinki: Ministry of Education and Culture. Accessed 30 September 2020. https://minedu.fi/en/comprehensive-school.

Morris, P. (ed.). *The Bakhtin Reader: Selected Writings of Bakhtin, Medvedev, and Voloshinov*. London: Edward Arnold.

Motro, D. and A. P. J. Ellis. 2017. 'Boys, Don't Cry: Gender and Reactions to Negative Performance Feedback'. *Journal of Applied Psychology* 102: 227–35. http://dx.doi.org/10.1037/apl0000175.

Mwiine, A. A. 2020. 'COVID-19 Global Disruptions and the Changing Masculinities: Critical Reflections from Uganda'. Accessed 8 March 2020. https://medium.com/@greatagresearch/covid-19-global-dis

ruptions-and-the-changing-masculinities-critical-reflections-from-uganda-8db19e0aa926.

Myllyniemi, S. 2009. *Aika vapaalla: nuorten vapaa-aikatutkimus 2009.* Helsinki: Valtion nuorisoasiain neuvottelukunta & Nuorisotutkimusseura.

Myllyniemi, S. 2014. *Ihmisarvoinen nuoruus. Nuorisobarometri 2014.* Helsinki: Nuorisotutkimusseura.

Myllyniemi, S. and P. Berg. 2013. *Nuoria liikkeellä! Nuorten vapaa-aikatutkimus 2013.* Helsinki: Opetus- ja kulttuuriministeriö, Valtion nuorisoneuvosto, Nuorisoasiain neuvottelukunta & Nuorisotutkimusverkosto.

Nayak, A. 2007. 'Critical Whiteness Studies'. *Sociology Compass* 1(2): 737–55. https://doi.org/10.1111/j.1751-9020.2007.00045.x.

Nicholas, L. and C. Agius. 2017. *The Persistence of Global Masculinism: Discourse, Gender and Neo-colonial Re-articulations of Violence.* Cham: Palgrave Macmillan/Springer.

Nielsen, H. B. and M. Rudberg. 1994. *Psychological Gender and Modernity.* Oslo: Universitetsforlaget.

O'Connor, P., A. Haynes and C. Kane. 2004. 'Relational Discourses. Social Ties with Family and Friends'. *Childhood* 11(3): 361–82. https://doi.org/10.1177/0907568204044888.

Odenbring, Y. and T. Johansson. 2021. 'Just a Joke? The Thin Line between Teasing, Harassment and Violence among Teenage Boys in Lower Secondary School'. *The Journal of Men's Studies* 29(2): 177–93. https://doi.org/10.1177/1060826520934771.

Oeur, F. B. 2018. *Black Boys Apart: Racial Uplift and Respectability in All-Male Public Schools.* Minneapolis, MN: University of Minnesota Press.

Official Statistics of Finland (OSF). 2019. 'Providers of Education and Educational Institutions. Educational institutions 2005–2019'. Accessed 6 January 2021. http://pxnet2.stat.fi/PXWeb/pxweb/en/StatFin/StatFin__kou__kjarj/statfin_kjarj_pxt_125j.px.

Official Statistics of Finland (OSF). 2021. *Population Structure.* Helsinki: Statistics Finland. Accessed 11 June 2021. http://www.stat.fi/til/vaerak/index_en.html.

Oransky, M. and J. Marecek. 2009. '"I'm Not Going to Be a Girl" Masculinity and Emotions in Boys' Friendships and Peer Groups'. *Journal of Adolescent Research* 24(2): 218–41. https://doi.org/10.1177/0743558408329951.

Orellana, M. E. F. 2019. *Mindful Ethnography: Mind, Heart and Activity for Transformative Social Research*. New York: Routledge.

Pascoe, C. J. 2005. '"Dude, You're a Fag": Adolescent Masculinity and the Fag Discourse'. *Sexualities* 8(3): 329–46. https://doi.org/10.1177/1363460705053337.

Pease, B. 2012. 'The Politics of Gendered Emotions: Disrupting Men's Emotional Investment in Privilege'. *Australian Journal of Social Issues* 47(1): 125–42. https://doi.org/10.1002/j.1839-4655.2012.tb00238.x.

Peltola, M. 2018. 'Tunteet rodullistettujen vähemmistöjen sukupolvisuhteissa'. In *Perhe ja tunteet*, edited by P. Eerola and H. Pirskanen, 111–29. Helsinki: Gaudeamus.

Peltola, M. 2020. 'Ristiriitainen maskuliinisuuskerronta ja tunteiden jakamisen mahdollisuudet poikien läheissuhteissa'. *Sosiologia* 57(1): 65–81.

Peltola, M. 2021. 'Everyday Consequences of Selectiveness. Borderwork in the Informal Sphere of a Lower Secondary School in the Metropolitan Area of Helsinki, Finland'. *British Journal of Sociology of Education* 42(1): 97–112. https://doi.org/10.1080/01425692.2020.1861930.

Peltola, M., S. Keskinen, V. Honkasalo and P. Honkatukia. 2017. 'Intergenerational Negotiations on (Hetero)sexuality and Romantic Relationships – Views of Young People and Parents in Multi-Ethnic Contexts'. *Journal of Youth Studies* 20(5): 533–48. https://doi.org/10.1080/13676261.2016.1241870.

Peltola, M. and A. Kivijärvi. 2017. 'Sport and Structured Leisure as Sites of Victimization for Children and Young People in Finland: Looking at the Significance of Gender and Ethnicity'. *International Review for Sociology of Sport* 52(8): 955–71. https://doi.org/10.1177/1012690216636607.

Peltola, M. and A. Phoenix. 2018. 'Sukupuolinäkökulma ja intersektionaalisuus: 11–14-vuotiaiden poikien maskuliinisuudet koulussa'. *Kasvatus* 49(3): 225–31.

Peltola, M. and A. Phoenix. 2022. 'Doing Whiteness and Masculinities at School: Finnish 12–15-Year-Olds' Narratives on Multiethnicity.' In *Finnishness, Whiteness and Coloniality*, edited by J. Hoegaerts, E. Peterson, T. Liimatainen and L. Hekanaho. Helsinki: Helsinki University Press.

Phoenix, A. 2008. 'Analysing Narrative Contexts'. In *Doing Narrative Research*, edited by M. Andrews, C. Squire and M. Tamboukou, 64–77. London: Sage.

Phoenix, A., J. Brannen, H. Elliott, J. Smithson, P. Morris, C. Smart, … and Bauer, E. 2016. 'Group Analysis in Practice: Narrative Approaches'. *Forum Qualitative Sozialforschung/Forum: Qualitative Social Research* 17(2). https://doi.org/10.17169/fqs-17.2.2391.

Phoenix, A. and P. Pattynama. 2006. 'Intersectionality'. *European Journal of Women's Studies* 13(3): 187–92. https://doi.org/10.1177/1350506806065751.

Pinkett, M. and M. Roberts. 2019. *Boys Don't Try? Rethinking Masculinity in Schools*. London: Routledge.

PISA15. 'Excellent Despite the Drop'. 2015. Helsinki: Ministry of Education and Culture. Accessed 10 June 2021. https://julkaisut.valtioneuvosto.fi/bitstream/handle/10024/79052/pisa15en.pdf?sequence=4&isAllowed=y.

PISA18. 'First Results – Finland among Top Performers'. 2018. Helsinki: Ministry of Education and Culture. Accessed 10 June 2021. https://julkaisut.valtioneuvosto.fi/bitstream/handle/10024/161921/PISA%2018%20first%20results%20-%20Brochure.pdf.

'Population with Foreign Background in Helsinki'. 2021. Helsinki: City of Helsinki. Accessed 28 August 2021. https://ulkomaalaistaustaisethelsingissa.fi/en/content/population-foreign-background-helsinki.

Puronaho, K. 2014. *Drop-out vai throw-out? Tutkimus lasten ja nuorten liikuntaharrastusten kustannuksista*. Helsinki: Ministry of Education and Culture.

Ralph, B. and S. Roberts. 2020. 'One Small Step for Man: Change and Continuity in Perceptions and Enactments of Homosocial Intimacy among Young Australian Men'. *Men and Masculinities* 23(1): 83–103. https://doi.org/10.1177/1097184X18777776.

Rastas, A. 2007. *Rasismi lasten ja nuorten arjessa*. Tampere: Tampere University Press.

Rattansi, A. and A. Phoenix. 2005. 'Rethinking Youth Identities: Modernist and Postmodernist Frameworks'. *Identity* 5(2): 97–123. https://doi.org/10.1207/s1532706xid0502_2.

Ravn, S. 2018. '"I Would Never Start a Fight but…" Young Masculinities, Perceptions of Violence, and Symbolic Boundary Work in Focus Groups'. *Men and Masculinities* 21(2): 291–309. https://doi.org/10.1177/1097184X17696194.

Reay, D. 2007. '"Unruly Places" : Inner-city Comprehensives, Middle-class Imaginaries and Working-class Children'. *Urban Studies* 44(7): 1191–1201. doi:10.1080/00420980701302965

Reeser, T. W. and L. Gottzén. 2018. 'Masculinity and Affect: New Possibilities, New Agendas'. *NORMA International Journal for Masculinity Studies* 13(3–4): 145–57. https://doi.org/10.1080/18902138.2018.1528722.

Reichert, M. C. and A. Keddie. 2019. 'Helping Schools Foster Healthy Masculinities'. *Men and Masculinities* 22(5): 914–16. https://doi.org/10.1177/1097184X19875493.

Renold, E. 2004. '"Other" Boys: Negotiating Non-hegemonic Masculinities in Primary School'. *Gender and Education* 16(2): 247–65. https://doi.org/10.1080/09540250310001690609.

Ribbens McCarthy, J. 2012. 'The Powerful Relational Language of "Family": Togetherness, Belonging and Personhood'. *The Sociological Review* 60(1): 68–90. https://doi.org/10.1111/j.1467-954X.2011.02045.x.

Riessman, C. K. 2008. *Narrative Methods for the Human Sciences*. London: Sage.

Ringrose, J. and E. Renold 2012. 'Slut-Shaming, Girl Power and "Sexualisation": Thinking through the Politics of the International SlutWalks with Teen Girls'. *Gender and Education* 24(3): 333–43. https://doi.org/10.1080/09540253.2011.645023.

Roberts, S. 2013. 'Boys Will Be Boys… Won't They? Change and Continuities in Contemporary Young Working-Class Masculinities'. *Sociology* 47(4): 671–86. https://doi.org/10.1177/0038038512453791.

Roberts, S. and K. Elliott. 2020. 'Challenging Dominant Representations of Marginalised Boys and Men in Critical Studies on Men and Masculinities'. *Boyhood Studies* 13(2): 87–104. https://doi.org/10.3167/bhs.2020.130207.

Salter, M. 2019. 'The Problem with a Fight Against Toxic Masculinity'. *The Atlantic*, 27. Accessed 5 January 2021. https://dickkesslerphd.com/wp-content/uploads/2019/03/The-Problem-With-a-Fight-Against-Toxic-Masculinity.pdf.

Santiago-Menendez, M. and A. Campbell. 2013. 'Sadness and Anger: Boys, Girls, and Crying in Adolescence'. *Psychology of Men and Masculinity* 14(4): 400–10. https://doi.org/10.1037/a0030661.

Sedgwick, E. K. 1985. *Between Men: Male Homosocial Desire and English Literature*. New York: Columbia University Press.

Souto, A-M. 2011. *Arkipäivän rasismi koulussa. Etnografinen tutkimus suomalais- ja maahanmuuttajanuorten ryhmäsuhteista*. Helsinki: Nuorisotutkimusseura.

Squire, C. 2008. 'Experience-Centred and Culturally-Oriented Approaches to Narrative'. In *Doing Narrative Research*, edited by M. Andrews, C. Squire and M. Tamboukou, 41–63. London: Sage.

Swain, J. 2000. '"The Money's Good, The Fame's Good, The Girls are Good": The Role of Playground Football in the Construction of Young Boys' Masculinity in a Junior School'. *British Journal of Sociology of Education* 21(1): 95–109. https://doi.org/10.1080/01425690095180.

Tarabini, A. and N. Ingram, eds. 2018. *Educational Choices, Transitions and Aspirations in Europe: Systemic, Institutional and Subjective Challenges*. London: Routledge.

Tervonen, M. 2014. 'Historiankirjoitus ja myytti yhden kulttuurin Suomesta'. In *Kotiseutu ja kansakunta – Miten suomalaista historiaa on rakennettu*, edited by P. Markkola, H. Snellman, and A.C. Östman, 137–62. Helsinki: Finnish Literature Society.

Thorne, B. 1993. *Gender Play. Girls and Boys in School.* Buckingham: Open University.

Tolonen, T. 2001. *Nuorten äänet ja tilat. Sukupuolten järjestykset koulun arjessa*. Helsinki: Gaudeamus.

Tolonen, T. 2008. 'Yhteiskuntaluokka: menneisyyden dinosauruksen luiden kalinaa?' In *Yhteiskuntaluokka ja sukupuoli*, edited by T. Tolonen, 8–17. Tampere: Vastapaino.

Tolonen, T. 2013. 'Youth Cultures, Lifestyles and Social Class in Finnish Contexts'. *YOUNG – Nordic Journal of Youth Research* 21(1): 55–75. https://doi.org/10.1177/1103308812467671.

Tolonen, T. 2017. 'Young People and Local Power Geometries in Helsinki. The Intertwining of Social Class, Gender and Ethnicity in Public Spaces'. In *Second International Handbook of Urban Education*, edited by W.T. Pink and G.W. Noblit, 755–74. Cham: Springer.

Törrönen, J. and F. Roumeliotis. 2014. 'Masculinities of Drinking as Described by Swedish and Finnish Age-Based Focus Groups'. *Addiction Research and Theory* 22(2): 126–36. https://doi.org/10.3109/16066359.2013.785533.

Tucker, L. A. and K. Govender. 2017. '"Sticks and Stones": Masculinities and Conflict Spaces'. *Gender and Education* 29(3): 352–68. https://doi.org/10.1080/09540253.2016.1156059.

Turtiainen, P., S. Karvonen and O. Rahkonen. 2007. 'All in the Family? The Structure and Meaning of Family Life among Young People'. *Journal of Youth Studies* 10(4): 477–93. https://doi.org/10.1080/13676260701262889.

UNHCR (The UN Refugee Agency). 2015. '2015: The Year of Europe's Refugee Crisis'. Accessed 10 June 2021. https://www.unhcr.org/news/stories/2015/12/56ec1ebde/2015-year-europes-refugee-crisis.html.

Vaattovaara, M., A. Joutsiniemi, M. Kortteinen, M. Stjernberg and T. Kemppainen. 2018. 'Experience of a Preventive Experiment: Spatial Social Mixing in Post-World War II Housing Estates in Helsinki, Finland'. In *Housing Estates in Europe: Poverty, Ethnic Segregation and Policy Challenges*, edited by D. Baldwin Hess, T. Tammaru and M. van Ham, 215–40. Cham: Springer.

Vettenranta, J., J. Välijärvi, A. Ahonen, J. Hautamäki, J. Hiltunen, K. Leino, S. Lähteinen, K. Nissinen, V. Nissinen, E. Puhakka, J. Rautopuro and M-P. Vainikainen. 2016. *PISA 2015: ensituloksia. Huipulla pudotuksesta huolimatta*. Helsinki: Ministry of Education and Culture.

Välijärvi, J. 2017. 'PISA 2015. Oppilaiden hyvinvointi'. Jyväskylä: Finnish Institute for Educational Research.

Waling, A. 2019. 'Rethinking Masculinity Studies: Feminism, Masculinity, and Poststructural Accounts of Agency and Emotional Reflexivity'. *Journal of Men's Studies* 27(1): 89–107. https://doi.org/10.1177/1060826518782980.

Wallenius, T. 2020. *Schools, Performance and Publicity. Contrasting the Policy on Publicising School Performance Indicators in Finland with the Other Nordic Countries*. Helsinki: University of Helsinki.

Ward, M. R. 2015. *From Labouring to Learning: Working-Class Masculinities, Education and De-industrialization*. Basingstoke: Palgrave Macmillan.

Ward, M. R. and T. Thurnell-Read. 2019. 'Boyhood and Belonging'. *Boyhood Studies* 12(2): 1–10. https://doi.org/10.3167/bhs.2019.120201.

Way, N. 2004. 'Intimacy, Desire, and Distrust in the Friendships of Adolescent Boys'. In *Adolescent boys* (pp. 167–196). New York University Press.

Way, N. 2011. *Deep Secrets*. Cambridge, MA: Harvard University Press.

Way, N. 2019. 'Reimagining Boys in the 21st Century'. *Men and Masculinities* 22(5): 926–29. https://doi.org/10.1177/1097184X19875170.

Way, N., J. Cressen, S. Bodian, J. Preston, J. Nelson and D. Hughes. 2014. '"It Might Be Nice to Be a Girl… Then You Wouldn't Have to Be Emotionless": Boys Resistance to Norms of Masculinity During Adolescence'. *Psychology of Men and Masculinity* 15(3): 241–52. https://doi.org/10.1037/a0037262.

Way, N. and J. Y. Chu. 2004. *Adolescent Boys: Exploring Diverse Cultures of Boyhood*. New York: NYU Press.

Wengraf, T. 2001. *Qualitative Research Interviewing: Biographic Narrative and Semi-structured Methods*. London: Sage.

Wenham, C., J. Smith and R. Morgan. 2020. 'Covid-19 Is an Opportunity for Gender Equality within the Workplace and at Home'. *BMJ* 369.

West, C. and S. Fenstermaker. 1993. 'Power, Inequality, and the Accomplishment of Gender: An Ethnomethodological View'. In *Theory on Gender/Feminism on Theory*, edited by P. England, 151–74. New York: Aldine.

Wetherell, M. 1998. 'Positioning and Interpretative Repertoires: Conversation Analysis and Post-structuralism in Dialogue'. *Discourse & Society* 9(3): 387–412. https://doi.org/10.1177/0957926598009003005.

Wetherell, M. 2012. *Affect and Emotion: A New Social Science Understanding*. London: Sage.

Wetherell, M. and N. Edley. 1999. 'Negotiating Hegemonic Masculinity: Imaginary Positions and Psycho-discursive Practices'. *Feminism & Psychology* 9(3): 335–56. https://doi.org/10.1177/0959353599009003012.

Wetherell, M. and N. Edley. 2014. 'A Discursive Psychological Framework for Analyzing Men and Masculinities'. *Psychology of Men and Masculinity* 15(4): 355–64. https://doi.org/10.1037/a0037148.

Willis, P. 1977. *Learning to Labour. How Working Class Kids Get Working Class Jobs*. Farnborough: Saxon House.

Wilson, S., S. Cunningham-Burley, A. Bancroft, K. Backett-Milburn. 2012. 'The Consequences of Love: Young People and Family Practices in Difficult Circumstances'. *The Sociological Review* 60(1): 110–28. https://doi.org/10.1111/j.1467-954X.2011.02049.x.

Yang, Y. 2020. 'What's Hegemonic about Hegemonic Masculinity? Legitimation and Beyond'. *Sociological Theory* 38(4): 318–33. https://doi.org/10.1177/0735275120960792.

YLE. 23.9.2020. 'Vanhemmat huolissaan Suomen kouluväkivallasta: "Kenelläkään koulun aikuisella ei ole lupa katsoa pois"'. YLE Uutiset. Accessed 4 January 2021. https://yle.fi/uutiset/3-11558790.

Yuval-Davis, N. 2011. *The Politics of Belonging: Intersectional Contestations*. London: Sage.

# Index

## E



## F



## G



## H

CPSIA information can be obtained
at www.ICGtesting.com
Printed in the USA
LVHW080318100422
715792LV00005B/413

9 789523 690660